Walks

MW00992660

Walking As An Aesthetic Practice

Francesco Careri

Culicidae
Architectural Press

Culicidae Architectural Press
an imprint of Culicidae Press, LLC
922 5TH ST
Ames, IA 50010
USA
www.culicidaepress.com
editor@culicidaepress.com
+1 (352) 388-3848
+1 (515) 462-0278

Culicidae
Architectural Press
Ames | Gainesville | Lemgo | Rome

WALKSCAPES: WALKING AS AN AESTHETIC PRACTICE
Published originally by Editorial Gustavo Gili, Barcelona, 2002
© Francesco Careri / Editorial Gustavo Gili, SL, Barcelona, 2002
And for the current edition,
© Culicidae Press, Ames, IA, 2017
© Introduction: Gilles Tiberghien
© English translation: Steven Piccolo
© Foreword: Christopher Flynn
© Interior and cover design: polytekton

ISBN-13:   978-1-68315-008-4

to Zonzo, with affection

Contents

Christopher Flynn

Foreword (2017)

The planners who designed the roads flowing south from Calais never imagined pedestrians. The pebbled pavement is gravel and sand strewn, and sidewalks make only occasional appearances. The houses and businesses one passes are not designed for the eye of the passerby. When William Wordsworth walked from the northern tip of France to the Alps in 1790 on the eve of the first anniversary of the fall of the Bastille, he first found himself in "a mean city," where he saw "How bright a face is worn when joy of one / Is joy for tens of millions." From there he headed south for the Alps:

> direct through hamlets, towns,
> Gaudy with reliques of that festival,
> Flowers left to wither on triumphal arcs,
> And window-garlands. On the public roads,
> And, once, three days successively, through paths
> By which our toilsome journey was abridged,
> Among sequestered villages we walked
> And found benevolence and blessedness
> Spread like a fragrance everywhere, when spring
> Hath left no corner of the land untouched …

A summer ago I went looking for roads through the countryside Wordsworth hurried across on his way to gaze at Mont Blanc. I had not read Francesco Careri's *Walkscapes* yet.

But after coming across it right after that journey, which involved a lot of imitation and repetition, it became clear to me that it spoke directly to that act of walking across the sad streets south of that mean city just across the channel from Dover. Careri traces a genealogy of walking across the twentieth century here, but the aggregate does more than that. This is a smart book, and more importantly, a useful one for those interested in what it means to walk through the banal cityscapes and suburbs of a world whose relationship to urbanism is once more in the midst of radical change. My walk from Calais to the Alps was intended as a re-creation for a documentary film project, but after reading *Walkscapes* I realized, or rather decided, it was its own errance, as much an architectural act as a pilgrimage. In other works, this book changed my mind, giving me a richer way of seeing an experience already filled with interesting complications.

Near the end of *Walkscapes*, Careri throws out the names of a few cities the Stalker Group has walked in acts he and they call 'transurbance.' "Losing itself amidst urban amnesias Stalker has encountered those spaces Dada defined as banal and those places the Surrealists defined as the unconscious of the city." Careri focuses on Robert Smithson's walks across an area most would consider an anti-landscape aggressively projecting an anti-aesthetic, the crumbling outskirts of Passaic, N.J., in the 1960s. For me, the focus on Smithson, a Minimalist artist, and his work in the late 1960s, spins a thread in the web of connections that make up *Walkscapes* and its explorations into walking as art that brings Wordsworth and the group of walkers he inspired into the same conversation. My failed attempt to follow in Wordsworth's footsteps—the roads aren't the same, and even if some of them are, they're paved, and run along canals dug long after the poet made his walk, across a landscape that has been radically changed and changed again—brought me to a landscape that reminded me of the New Jersey where I grew up, and the Passaic that figures prominently in Careri's account of those whose footsteps he identifies as antecedents.

So when I call this book 'useful,' I mean that it has helped me tease out some of the things I have been trying to think about walks I have been making that connect my suburban New Jersey boyhood to my intentional failures to repeat the walks British Romantic poets made in the late eighteenth and early nineteenth centuries. At a time when cities all over the world have been re-urbanizing after having emptied out in the last decades in the twentieth century, this book and its focus on how we encounter the cityscape cover similar ground to that touched by Kierkegaard in *Repetition* (1843), a book about the impossibility of recreating any experience. Kierkegaard has a perfect night at the theater, watching the play, sitting in a box with a view of other spectators who form a tableau that strikes him as perfect. The next night he returns, but the play is not exactly the same, the people in the boxes around him do not arouse the same interest, and from this he develops the idea that experiences are unique, no matter how one tries to recreate them. I knew this with the walks I took throughout Europe, so failure was built into my expectations. Careri's focus here on Smithson and his experiments in Passaic, a town where I worked for a newspaper and lived, and his own recursive walks across European cities that have been walked by previous artists, brought about a set of connections in my mind that made sense of it all. Not a communicable kind of sense, but one that somehow put Passaic, Calais, Wordsworth, Kierkegaard and the idea of the Walkscape into a functional harmony.

Errare humanum est, Careri reminds us, going back to an early history of walkers as architects, to nomads in story and reality. To err means to wander, and to wander is to leave the path, and before long, to go wrong. Like many writers who have tackled the concept of nomadism throughout time, Careri recounts the tale of Cain and Abel, but in this book he brings out the complications of Cain's story. The first murderer may have been the first nomad, but before that, he was the first farmer, and his brother was the first shepherd. The move from pastoral life to nomadic travel initiates the kinds of moves this book examines throughout the twentieth century. Nomads in the strictest sense aren't aimless. They bring cattle to market, goods to a place of trading, families to food and water. In this sense of the term, to err is human because to wander is often necessary for humanity. Careri doesn't let the reader forget that not only are the wanderings of Cain human, but Cain's work at building the first city, Enoch, was also a natural impulse, and the acts of modern wanderers who carve constantly disappearing paths through cities are both natural and an art form.

Francesco Careri (2017)

Compared with the first edition of this book there have not been any substantive changes. My text and the introduction by Gilles Tiberghien remain in the original translation made by Steven Piccolo. However, this latest version has been expanded and upgraded in the notes and the bibliography sections. It begins with the new foreword by Christopher Flynn, my epilogue for the second Spanish edition, and it ends with the Stalker Manifesto written by Lorenzo Romito as a tribute to Stalker from *Walkscapes*. I want to thank Mikesch Muecke for republishing it with Culicidade Press.

With respect to the layout of the book, the gray pages will allow the reader to access an important amount of heterogeneous materials. These are quotes, photographs, flyers, press releases, poems, maps, glossaries, thematic inserts, and stories. The book can be read only through those documents, which are basically the few testimonials of those who worried more about walking than leaving traces.

Walkscapes Ten Years Later (2013)

I have often thought about writing a second book on walking, and about updating *Walkscapes* with new chapters on artists who make walking part of their work today. If I have refrained, it is because I think the book works just as it is, and because I don't believe I can do much better on this theme. So the text of this new edition is exactly the same as the original; I haven't changed a single letter. There are a few more footnotes, given the fact that I had already added some for the Italian edition, and I have removed a few of the illustrations, because they seemed superfluous. The bibliography has been updated, because in recent years much has been written on this theme. And I have decided to write this short preface which, perhaps in an overly autobiographical, introspective way, attempts to explain how I have myself interpreted the words written at the end of the book:

> Venturing into New Babylon can be a useful method for the interpretation and transformation of those zones of Zonzo that, in recent years, have thrown the disciplines of architecture and urban planning into crisis. And thanks to the artists who have roamed its interior, this city is visible today and appears as one of the most important unresolved problems of architectural culture. To design a nomadic city would seem to be a contradiction in terms. Perhaps it must be done in keeping with the manner of the Neo-Babylonians: transforming it playfully from the inside out, modifying it during the journey, restoring life to the primitive aptitude for the play of relations that permitted Abel to dwell in the world.

Many things have happened over the last ten years: three children, from whom I learn every day to play with the world; a position at the university, where I teach a course entirely based on walking; the house-manifesto built together with the descendants of Abel and then burned down by Cain and his anti-tzigane cohorts; and the Laboratory of Civic Arts, with which I move forward with the collective projects I previously did with Stalker, and which ideally continues to follow the path of Stalker.

Ten years ago, when Daniela Colafranceschi and Monica Gili asked me to write the book, I would never have imagined it would be reprinted six times, and reissued in this new form. I actually had no idea what it meant to write a book, to put statements on paper that I would then have to confirm, discuss, elaborate, defend. Above all, I had no idea a book could make me travel so extensively. *Walkscapes*, especially in South America, has met with unexpected success, and I have been invited to conferences and seminars, and above all to walk with artists, architects, students, citizens. Crossing Bogota, Santiago, Montevideo, São Paulo, Salvador da Bahia, Talca, I have understood that I don't know how to walk in the colonial *grid* and that to cross the city, in a 'transurbance,' I have to look for the points in which the grid breaks up, lose my way along rivers, skirting around the new residential zones, plunging into the mazes of the favelas. Walking in South America means coming to terms with many fears: fear of the city, fear of public space, fear of breaking rules, fear of usurping space, fear of crossing often non-existent barriers, fear of other inhabitants, nearly always perceived as potential enemies. To put it simply, walking is scary, so people don't walk any more; those who walk are homeless, drug addicts, outcasts. The anti-peripatetic and anti-urban phenomenon is clearer here than in Europe, where it still seems to only be on the verge of taking form: never leave the house on foot, never expose your body without an enclosure, protect it in the home or in the car. Above all, never go out after sundown! Shut yourself up, if possible, in gated communities to watch terrifying films or to travel with the Internet. Commit advertising to memory so you will know what to look for when you're strolling in shopping malls. At architecture schools I realized that the students, the future ruling class, know everything about urban theory and French philosophers; they say they are experts on cities and public space, but actually they have never had the experience of playing soccer in the street, of meeting friends at the square, of making out in a park, or sneaking into an industrial ruin, crossing a favela, stopping to ask a stranger for directions. What kind of city could ever produce these people who are scared of walking?

The only category with which cities are designed today is that of security. It might sound banal, but the only way to have a safe city is to have people walking in the street. This factor alone allows people to watch and watch out for each other, without any need for fences and surveillance cameras. And the only way to have a living, democratic city is to be able to walk, without erasing conflicts and differences, to be able to walk to protest, to reassert our *right to the city*. As a teacher I feel I have more responsibilities, and I have begun to understand that walking is an indispensable tool to train not only students but also citizens, that walking is an action capable of lowering the level of fear and of unmasking the media construct of insecurity: a 'civic' project that is able to produce public space and common action. In my Civic Arts courses what I try to transmit to the students is the pleasure of getting lost for the sake of knowledge. The outcome cannot be taken for granted, but it brings remarkable rewards. I take them where they've never been as yet, I pull the rug out from under their feet and highjack them into uncharted territories. Usually at the beginning there's a mood of reluctance and distrust, doubts about what we are doing, the fear of wasting time. But in the end, for those who stick with it, there is the growing pleasure of finding new paths and new certainties, of building thought with your own body, acting with your own mind. Casting doubt on the few certainties you have just managed to put together thus far is actually a way to open the mind to previously unexplored worlds and possibilities, encouraging you to reinvent everything, from scratch: your idea of the city, your own definition of art and architecture, your own place in this world. You can break free of false convictions and start to remember that space is a fantastic invention with which you can play, like a kid. One motto that guides our walks is "lose time to gain space." If we want to gain 'other' spaces we have to know how to play, to deliberately get out of a functional-productive system in order to enter a non-functional, unproductive system. You have to learn how to lose time, not always seeking the shortest route, letting yourself get detoured by events, heading towards more impenetrable paths where it is possible to 'stumble,' maybe even to get stuck, talking with the people you meet or knowing how to stop, forgetting that you were supposed to proceed; to know how to achieve unintentional walking, indeterminate walking.

Another passage has been that of a deeper understanding of the term *dérive* (drift) in the sense of an "indeterminate project" and its potential for the transformation of the *nomadic*—or more precisely *informal*—city. Therefore the term is seen not only in its meaning of "letting oneself go adrift," of getting lost, at the mercy of the currents, but also in a more *project*-ive sense, as a tool to "construct a direction:" a "playful-constructive situation" (Debord), "to make in the form of a dynamic labyrinth together with the inhabitants of New Babylon" (Constant). What appeals to me about the seagoing metaphor of drift is that the land on which we move is indeed an uncertain sea that constantly changes based on the shifting of winds, currents, our moods, our encounters. The point, in fact, is how to designate a direction, but with extensive openness to indeterminacy, and to listen to the projects of others. Helming a sailboat means constructing a route and continuously adjusting it, reading the ripples on the sea, seeking zones with gusts and avoiding doldrums. In short, finding the energies, in the territory and the people that inhabit it, that can take an indeterminate project forward in its becoming: the right people, the right places and situations in which the project can grow, change, and become common ground. It is clear that if we have a determinate project, it will only fall to pieces at the first gusts of wind. There are definitely greater hopes of achieving an indeterminate project.

What we have said thus far has a lot to do with 'relational' or 'participatory' creative processes, both words that have been sorely abused of late in the world of art and architecture; let's say that they are creative processes that cannot meet fulfillment without an exchange with the Other. In these situations, the operation usually happens in one of two ways: either you get the 'other' involved in your own project, to obtain consensus, or you cancel out your own creativity, leaving the completion of the work completely up to the other. Instead, I believe it is interesting to navigate between these two shores, aware of the fact that we have our own creative project (even our desire to participate is a project in its own right), but also knowing that we want to leave it open, indeterminate. The steering will therefore be done by the inner coherence between the things we come across and those we create, between things that happen and things we make happen, the ongoing discovery of a hidden order we can observe as it comes to life beneath our feet and the perspective they afford us, the possibility of constructing a meaning and a coherent, shared story-route.

At the beginning I mentioned a house-manifesto made with the descendants of Abel, the so-called 'nomads.' This was Savorengo Ker ("the house of all" in the Romané language), built together with the Romani of the Casilino 900 camp in Rome in July 2008. It was supposed to be the first step in the transformation of the Romani camp into a neighborhood, a city piece, maybe an unstable *Sahel* between nomadism and steady settlement. After writing the book, the word 'nomadism' has taken on many other meanings for me. I began to spend time with people who have firsthand experience of nomadism, not by choice or cultural tradition: those who have had to give up and live in the apartheid of migrant camps, those who still try to inhabit the world in a totally free way but run into infinite barriers to movement. The story of the Savorengo Ker is long and very complex. Perhaps one day I will be able to write a book about it. In the meantime we have made a film, which I urge you to watch on the web. But what I want to say right now is that this was an important phase of the 'indeterminate project.' The house's design did not come from a drawing but from an encounter, a mutual exchange of distrust and fears, then of knowledge and desires. Its idea, its form, its technology, its economics were continuously discussed, negotiated—sometimes heatedly—in a continuous open dialogue between a community of 'nomads' by now forced to remain in one place, and a variegated group of 'settlers,' stable residents with a passion for nomadism, indignant about the situation of apartheid that is now forcing the Romani into increasingly sophisticated concentration camps. The result was a wooden house with two levels, with imaginative Balkan decorations and a very ambitious project: to tell Cain that Abel too has the right to live in the intercultural city, and that his presence is a great boon precisely because it brings with it an age-old conflict that will never be pacified.

From this standpoint, I think the story of Cain and Abel and the gesture of the 'ka' still have much to teach to the arts that focus on the transformation of space. In the first chapter, we left off at the point when, after the first murder in the history of humankind, God punished Cain by banishing him to wander in the desert. I have never stopped wondering about Cain's reaction. His fear is not of getting lost, but of meeting the Other; he is afraid the Other will kill him, and his sole concern is how to approach that conflict. The Bible tells us God gave Cain a 'sign' to protect him. A mark? The mark of Cain? I began to study this, and it seems to me that in the imagery of Cain this sign does not appear; instead, he carries with him the walking stick of the wayfarer. I am becoming convinced that the Lord did not exactly "give a sign" (*signum*) to Cain, nor a walking stick, but instead "taught" (*insignare*) Cain to do something he did not know how to do. God taught Cain to greet, to go towards the Other making a non-belligerent 'sign.' And I am increasingly convinced that the greeting is the same as the 'ka' symbol (part of the etymology of the name Cain): two raised arms of a person walking towards you, approaching the Other, no longer to kill him as Cain had just done with his brother, but displaying empty hands, disarmed, unthreatening, reaching for an embrace. I am convinced that those who wrote the Book of Genesis understood that this first revolutionary act of peace was connected with walking and stopping. The art of wandering is followed by the art of meeting, of the construction of a threshold, the creation of a border outside Space and Time, in which to approach conflict between differences with a non-belligerent greeting.

Maybe I will begin my next book here. It might be called *Stopscapes. Stopping as an aesthetic practice.* I would like to stop talking about walking in order to lose one's way, and instead talk about walking to stumble on the Other, the decision to stop somewhere to construct a space of encounter among diversities, the birth of Kronos and the Space of Losing Time, the indeterminate project and participation as citizens in the hybrid evolutions of those New Babylons that already exist in our cities.

Rome, 4 August 2012

Gilles A. Tiberghien

Nomad City
Introduction to the Frst Edition (2002)

In *Walkscapes,* Francesco Careri does more than write a book on walking considered as a critical tool, an obvious way of looking at landscape, and as a form of emergence of a certain kind of art and architecture. Into the bargain he gives the Stalker group, originally made up of young student architects, a work that partly roots its activities in the past, gives it a genealogy in any event, as did André Breton when he considered Surrealism historically as a sort of comet's tail of German Romanticism, and as did the Jena Romantics themselves in their review of the *Athenaeüm* by annexing Chamfort, Cervantes or Shakespeare and declaring them to be premature Romantics. Or then again like Smithson in his text on Central Park, making its creator, Frederick Law Olmstead, an ancestor of Land Art.

More than the Surrealists—whom he nonetheless opportunely rereads here via André Breton's *Nadja* and *Mad Love,* or Louis Aragon's *Paris Peasant*—it is Dada and its outings in the capital, its random wanderings through the French countryside, that Francesco Careri claims kinship with. Nearer still to our own time, it's the Situationists that the Stalkers can be compared to. The two groups share a taste for urban investigation, and a sensitivity to contemporary change as being symptomatic of a society in a state of mutation, not to say 'decomposition.' They know how to scrutinize the unconscious of the city, as Benjamin once did in studying 19th-century Paris.

When Francesco Careri writes in "Rome archipel fractal" that "We've chosen the trajectory as a form of expression which accentuates a place by physically tracing a line through it. The act of traversal, an instrument of phenomenological knowledge and symbolic interpretation of the territory, is a form of psychogeographical reading of it comparable to the 'walkabout' of the Australian aborigenes," the references, be they implicit, are clear.[i]

But make no mistake about it: neither the Stalkers nor Francesco Careri are neo-Situationists. Stalker is a group, to be sure, but a completely informal one, and if Francesco Careri and Lorenzo Romito are its two most prolific theoreticians they have no final say in the matter. Furthermore, each member of the group knows what he or she owes to the others in the collective, the number of which varies momentarily between seven and twenty individuals. This is its fundamental difference with the avant-garde groups that sprang up in the 20th century, alternatively enrolling and excluding their members. We are faced, here, with an experimental praxis that avails itself of theoretical tools when and as they are needed, and always with a sense of appropriateness, something which gives it great suppleness and considerable intellectual mobility. Indeed, the group launched a manifesto in January 1996,[ii] but reading it quickly convinces us of its non-dogmatic quality and its essentially heuristic function. *Walkscapes* partakes of this same spirit. It gives point to a practice of which Stalker seeks to be the prolongation, the amplification, the adjustment, and—why not?—also the culmination, in a sense. Francesco Careri puts his researches, and also his theoretical inventiveness, at the disposition of the group. At the same time he offers us a rereading of the history of art in terms of the practice of walking (such as he conceives of it), from the erection of the menhirs, through Egypt and Ancient Greece, up to the protagonists of Land Art.

The anthropological, philosophic, sociopolitical, and artistic insights the author presents us with serve, at any one moment, a discourse of great lucidity, the ambition of which is to bring us up to today, to *Zonzo,* that purely linguistic place encountered in the expression *andare a Zonzo,* and which means drifting without a goal, as did the walker in the 19th-century city.

Such an expression is what's called a "fixed syntagm", one which may only conform to a timeless reality. Today the landmarks have disappeared: one no longer traverses *Zonzo* as before, with the guarantee of going from the center to the periphery. There was a time when the center was dense and the outskirts of the city increasingly dispersed; right now the center is riddled with empty spaces.

The idea suffusing the book as a whole, and which the author convincingly describes—and what does it matter if it's historically correct or not, as long as it's operative—is that walking has always generated architecture and landscape, and that this practice, all but totally forgotten by architects themselves, has been reactivated by poets, philosophers and artists capable of seeing precisely what is not there, in order to make 'something' be there. Hence, for instance, Emmanuel Hocquard and Michael Palmer, who in 1990 founded the *Museum of Negativity* after having spotted an immense hole beside the Autoroute du Nord in France. Or Gordon Matta-Clark, who in the 1970s bought up tiny bits of land in between almost touching buildings, and who declared that "through the 'negative space' a void exists so that the 'ingredients can be seen in a moving way or a dynamic way.'"[iii]

We find the inventory of a certain number of these attitudes, and the philosophical reflections elicited by walking, in a Bruce Chatwin book Careri often cites, *The Songlines,* a sort of paean to nomad thinking, more than to nomadism itself, it has to be said. By dynamizing them, the act of walking in fact makes the songlines crisscrossing Aborigine territory visible, those perspective lines which cleave the screen of the landscape in its most traditional representation, "witch lines," as Deleuze would say, that sweep thought along in the wake of the movement of things, along the veins the passing whales delineate at the bottom of the sea, described so well by Melville in *Moby–Dick.*

But the world Careri and his friends elect to explore is that of the urban changes wrought to what used to be called the countryside, and of which nothing more remains than a "holed" or "moth-eaten" reality—the author utilizes the image of a leopard skin "with empty spots in the built city and full spots in the heart of the countryside"—, a group of territories belonging to the suburbs, a word that, as Smithson explains, "literally means 'city below,'" and which he describes as "a circular abyss between town and country, a place where buildings seem to sink away from one's vision or buildings fall back into sprawling babels or limbos." There, he adds, "the landscape is effaced into sidereal expanses and contractions."[iv]

This notion is not—or no longer is—uniquely European: far from it, as the reference to Smithson demonstrates. One also thinks of John Brinckerhoff Jackson, a great observer of landscape, who was extremely interested in the traces and organization of roads across American territory, showing how, far from just traversing landscapes and built-up areas, they engendered new forms of inhabitable space, thus creating new kinds of sociability. "Roads no longer merely lead to places," he wrote, "they *are* places."[v] And so are the paths the Stalkers follow during their walks through "the city limits," far from the main communication routes. As it is, Jackson observed exactly the same thing as the group of Italian nomads: the formation of a new landscape that didn't correspond to either the one in the classical representations power had described or to their 'vernacular' form, which is what he preferred to scrutinize. This unprecedented landscape is created by roads, new habits of mobility and the transporting of goods previously stockpiled at home. It is characterized by mobility and change, and it is on the approaches to these thoroughfares that encounters, as well as an indubitably new type of mutual aid, occur. Thus, "churches used as discothèques, dwellings used as churches [...] one encounters empty spaces in the very heart of dense cities and industrial installations in the middle of the countryside."[vi]

The interstices and voids Careri observes, and which aren't just on the outskirts of the city but in its very center, are nevertheless occupied by 'marginal' populations who have invented branching systems that are largely unknown, unnoticed places that, because they are always shifting, come together, the author says, like a sea whose islets of dwellings would be the archipelagos. This image is a good one, since it illustrates the relative indeterminacy of these limits incurred by walking.

The 'marches' was the name traditionally given to territories situated at the confines of a territory, at the edges of its borders.[vii] Walking [*la marche*] also designates a shifting limit, which is nothing other, in fact, than what's called a frontier. The latter always goes hand in hand with fringes, intermediary spaces, with undeterminable contours that can only really be made out when travelling through them. It's walking, too, which makes the internal frontiers of the city evident, which, by identifying it, reveals the *zone.* Whence the beautiful title *Walk-scape,* which stresses the revelatory power of this dynamism mobilizing the entire body—social as well as individual—in order to then transform the mind of he who knows how to look. Such an enterprise has a genuine 'political' stake—in the primal sense of the word—a way of keeping art, urbanism and the social project at an equal, and sufficient, distance from each other in order to effectively illuminate these empty spaces we have such need of to *live well.*

Notes

[i] Francesco Careri, "Rome, archipel fractal. Voyage dans les combles de la ville," in *Techniques & Architecture*, 427, August-September 1996. "Psychogéographie: étude des effets précis du milieu géographique, consciemment aménagé ou non, agissant sur le comportement affectif des individus," in *Internationale Situationniste*, 1, June 1958, p. 13. (English version: Andreotti, Libero; Costa, Xavier (eds.), *Theory of The Dérive: Art, Politics, Urbanism,* Museu d'Art Contemporàni de Barcelona/Actar, Barcelona, 1996).

[ii] Republished in French and in Italian in *Stalker: À travers les territoires actuels,* Jean Michel Place, Paris, 2000.

[iii] Emmanuel Hocquard, "Taches blanches", in *Ma haie. Un privé à Tanger II,* P.O.L., Paris, 2001. V. A. [various authors] *Gordon Matta-Clark,* R.M.N., Marseilles, 1993.

[iv] Robert Smithson, "A Museum of Language in the Vicinity of Art," in *The Writings of Robert Smithson,* New York University Press, New York, 1979.

[v] John Brinckerhoff Jackson, *A Sense of Place, a Sense of Time,* Yale University Press, New Haven & London, 1994.

[vi] John Brinckerhoff Jackson, *Discovering the Vernacular Landscape,* Yale University Press, New Haven & London, 1984. I'm using here Luc Baboulet's translation from *Le Visiteur,* 6, 2000. One can relate this text to what Francesco Careri writes: "We've visited churches that resemble industrial hangars, abandoned factories similar to ruined cathedrals, Roman ruins in the state Goethe, Poussin or Piranesi saw them in." Cf. Francesco Careri, "Rome, archipel fractal," op. cit.

[vii] Cf. the suggestive book by Piero Zanini, *Significati del confine,* Mondadori, Milan, 2000.

To cross	a territory	to walk
To open	a path	
To recognize	a place	
To discover	propensities	
To attribute	aesthetic values	
To comprehend	symbolic values	
To invent	a geography	to get oriented
To assign	place names	
To descend	a ravine	
To climb	a mountain	
To trace	a form	
To draw	a point	
To tread	a line	to get lost
To inhabit	a circle	
To visit	a stone	
To narrate	a city	
To traverse	a map	
To perceive	sounds	
To guide oneself	through smells	to err
To observe	thorns	
To listen to	ditches	
To celebrate	dangers	
To navigate	a desert	
To sniff	a forest	
To breach	a continent	to submerge
To meet	an archipelago	
To host	an adventure	
To measure	a dump	
To grasp	elsewhere	
To populate	sensations	
To construct	relations	to wander
To find	objects	
To take	phrases	
To not take	bodies	
To tail	people	
To track	animals	
To enter	a hole	to penetrate
To interact with	a grating	
To hurdle	a wall	
To investigate	an enclosure	
To follow	an instinct	
To leave	a station platform	
To not leave	traces	to go forward

Walkscapes

The list on the facing page contains a series of actions that have only recently become part of the history of art. As a whole they can be a useful aesthetic tool with which to explore and transform the nomadic spaces of the contemporary city. Before erecting menhirs—known as *benben* in Egyptian, "the first stone that emerged from the chaos"—man possessed a symbolic form with which to transform the landscape. This form was walking, a skill learned with great effort in the first months of life, only to become an unconscious, natural, automatic action. It was by walking that man began to construct the natural landscape of his surroundings. And in our own century we have formulated the categories for interpreting the urban landscapes that surround us by walking through them.

Errare Humanum Est...

The act of crossing space stems from the natural necessity to move to find the food and information required for survival. But once these basic needs have been satisfied, walking takes on a symbolic form that has enabled man to dwell in the world. By modifying the sense of the space crossed, walking becomes man's first aesthetic act, penetrating the territories of chaos, constructing an order on which to develop the architecture of *situated objects*.

Walking is an art from whose loins spring the menhir, sculpture, architecture, landscape. This simple action has given rise to the most important relationships man has established with the land, the territory.

Nomadic transhumance, generally thought of as the archetype for any journey, was actually the development of the endless wanderings of hunters in the Paleolithic period, whose symbolic meanings were translated by the Egyptians in the *ka,* the symbol of *eternal wandering.* This primitive roving lived on in religion (the journey as ritual) and in literary forms (the journey as narrative), transformed as a sacred path, dance, pilgrimage, and procession. Only in the last century has the journey-path freed itself of the constraints of religion and literature to assume the status of a pure aesthetic act. Today it is possible to construct a history of walking as a form of urban intervention that inherently contains the symbolic meanings of the primal creative act: roaming as architecture of the landscape, where the term landscape indicates the action of symbolic as well as physical transformation of anthropic space.

This is the perspective in which we have taken a deeper look at three important moments of passage in art history—all absolutely familiar to historians—in which an experience linked to walking represented a turning point. These are the passages from Dada to Surrealism (1921-1924), from the Lettrist International to the Situationist International (1956-1957), and from Minimal Art to Land Art (1966-1967). By analyzing these episodes we simultaneously obtain a history of the roamed city that goes from the *banal city* of Dada to the *entropic city* of Robert Smithson, passing through the unconscious and *oneiric city* of the Surrealists and the *playful* and *nomadic city* of the Situationists. What the rovings of the artists discover is a liquid city, an amniotic fluid where the spaces of the *elsewhere* take spontaneous form, an urban archipelago in which to navigate by drifting. A city in which the *spaces of staying* are the islands in the great sea formed by the *space of going.*

Anti Walk

Walking was experienced for the entire first part of the 20th century as a form of anti-art. In 1921 Dada organized a series of "visit-excursions" to the banal places of the city of Paris. This was the first time art rejected its assigned places, setting out to reclaim urban space. The 'visit' was one of the tools selected by Dada to achieve that surpassing of art that was to become the red thread for any understanding of the subsequent avant-gardes. In 1924 the Parisian Dadaists organized trips in the open country. They discovered a dream-like, surreal aspect to walking and defined this experience as 'deambulation,' a sort of automatic writing in real space, capable of revealing the unconscious zones of space, the repressed memories of the city. At the beginning of the 1950s the Lettrist International, disputing Surrealist deambulation, began to construct that "Theory of Drifting" which, in 1956, at Alba, was to come into contact with the nomadic universe. In 1957 Constant designed a camp for the gypsies of Alba, while Asger Jorn and Guy Debord provided the first images of a city based on the *dérive*. Lettrist urban drifting was transformed into the construction of situations, experimenting with playful-creative behavior and unitary environments. Constant reworked Situationist theory to develop the idea of a nomadic city—New Babylon—bringing the theme of nomadism into the sphere of architecture and laying the groundwork for the radical avant-gardes of the years to follow.

Land Walk

The second half of the 20th century viewed walking as one of the forms used by artists to intervene in nature. In 1966 the magazine *Artforum* published the story of the journey of Tony Smith along a highway under construction. A controversy broke out between modernist critics and Minimalist artists. Certain sculptors began to explore the theme of the path, first as an object and later as an experience. Land Art re-examined, through walking, the archaic origins of landscape and the relationship between art and architecture, making sculpture reclaim the spaces and means of architecture. In 1967 Richard Long produced *A Line Made by Walking,* a line drawn by stepping on the grass in a field. The action left a trace on the land, the sculpted object was completely absent, and walking became an autonomous art form. That same year Robert Smithson made *A Tour of the Monuments of Passaic.* This was the first such voyage through the empty spaces of the contemporary urban periphery. The tour of the new monuments led Smithson to draw certain conclusions: the relationship between art and nature had changed, nature itself had changed, the contemporary landscape autonomously produced its own space, in the 'repressed' parts of the city we could find the abandoned futures produced by entropy.

Transurbance

The interpretation of the present city from the point of view of roaming is based on the 'transurbances' conducted by Stalker since 1995 in a number of European cities. Losing itself amidst urban amnesias Stalker has encountered those spaces Dada defined as *banal* and those places the Surrealists defined as the *unconscious of the city.* Repressed memory, rejection, and absence of control have produced a *system of empty spaces* (the sea of the archipelago) through which it is possible to drift, as in the labyrinthine sectors of Constant's New Babylon: a nomadic space ramified as a system of *urban sheep tracks* that seems to have taken form as the result of the entropy of the city, as one of the "forgotten futures" described by Robert Smithson. Inside the wrinkles of the city, spaces in transit have grown, territories in continuous transformation in time. These are the places where today it is possible to go beyond the age-old division between nomadic space and settled space.

Actually, nomadism has always existed in osmosis with settlement, and today's city contains nomadic spaces (*voids*) and sedentary spaces (*solids*) that exist side by side in a delicate balance of reciprocal exchange. Today the nomadic city lives inside the stationary city, feeding on its scraps and offering, in exchange, its own presence as a new nature that can be crossed only by inhabiting it.

Transurbance is, just like the erratic journey, a sort of pre-architecture of the contemporary landscape. The first aim of this book, therefore, is to reveal the falseness of any anti-architectural image of nomadism, and thus of walking: hunters of the Paleolithic period and nomadic shepherds are the origin of the *menhir,* the first object of the landscape from which architecture was developed. The landscape seen as an *architecture of open space* is an invention of the civilization of wandering. Only during the last ten thousand years of sedentary living have we passed from the architecture of open space to the architecture of filled space.

The second aim is to understand the place of the path-journey in the history of architectural archetypes. In this sense we must make a journey back to the roots of the relationship between path and architecture, and therefore between roaming and the menhir, in an age in which architecture did not exist as the physical construction of space, but as a symbolic construction—inside the path—of the territory.

Toward A New Expansion of The Field

The term 'path' simultaneously indicates the act of crossing (the path as the action of walking), the line that crosses the space (the path as architectural object) and the tale of the space crossed (the path as narrative structure). We intend to propose the path as an aesthetic form available to architecture and the landscape. In this century the rediscovery of the path happened first in literature (Tristan Tzara, André Breton, and Guy Debord are writers), then in sculpture (Carl Andre, Richard Long, and Robert Smithson are sculptors), while in the field of architecture the path has led to the pursuit of the historical foundations of radical anti-architecture in nomadism, and has not yet led to a positive development. Through the path different disciplines have produced their own "expansion of the field" (Rosalind Krauss) for coming to terms with their own limits. Retracing the margins of their disciplines, many artists have attempted not to fall into the abyss of negation consciously opened by Dada at the beginning of the 20th century, but to leap beyond it. Breton transformed the anti-art of Dada into Surrealism through an expansion of the field toward psychology; the Situationists, starting again from Dada, attempted to transform anti-art into a unified discipline (*urbanisme unitaire*) through the expansion of the field toward politics; Land Art transformed the sculptural object into construction of the territory by expanding the field toward landscape and architecture.

It has often been observed that the architectural discipline has, in recent years, expanded its field in the direction of sculpture and the landscape. In this direction we also find the crossing of space, seen not as a manifestation of anti-art but as an aesthetic form that has achieved the status of an autonomous discipline. Today architecture could expand into the field of the path without encountering the pitfalls of anti-architecture. The transurbance between the edges of the discipline and the place of exchange between the nomadic and the settled city can represent a first step. In this space of encounter walking is useful for architecture as a cognitive and design tool, as a means of recognizing a geography in the chaos of the peripheries, and a means through which to invent new ways to intervene in public metropolitan spaces, to investigate them and

Nomad "*Nomos* is Greek for 'pasture' and 'the Nomad' is a chief or clan elder who presides over the allocation of pastures. [...] The verb *nemein*–'to graze', 'to pasture', 'to range' or 'to spread'–has a second sense as early as Homer: 'to deal', 'to apportion' or 'to dispense'–especially of land, honor, meat or drink. *Nemesis* is the 'distribution of justice' and so of 'divine justice'. *Nomisma* means 'current coin': hence 'numismatics'. [...] In fact, almost all our monetary expressions–capital, stock, pecuniary, chattel, sterling–perhaps even the idea of 'growth' itself–have their origins in the pastoral world."

BRUCE CHATWIN, *The Songlines*, Viking, New York, 1987.

make them visible. The aim is not to encourage architects and landscape architects to leave their drawing boards behind, shouldering the backpack of nomadic transurbance, nor is it to theorize a total absence of paths to permit the citizen to get lost, although often *errare* could truly be seen as a *value* instead of an *error*. The aim is to indicate walking as an aesthetic tool capable of describing and modifying those metropolitan spaces that often have a nature still demanding comprehension, to be *filled with meanings* rather than designed and *filled with things*. Walking then turns out to be a tool which, precisely due to the simultaneous reading and writing of space intrinsic to it, lends itself to attending to and interacting with the mutability of those spaces, so as to intervene in their continuous becoming by acting in the field, in the *here and now* of their transformation, sharing from the inside in the mutations of these spaces that defy the conventional tools of contemporary design. Today architecture can transform the path from anti-architecture into a resource, expanding its field of disciplinary action toward something close by, taking a step in the direction of the path. The following reflections are intended to be a contribution in this direction.

"Much as the nomad trajectory follows habitual trails or paths, their function is not that of the sedentary path, which consists in *spreading human beings out in an enclosed space*, assigning each person his or her part and regulating communication between the parts. The nomad trajectory does the opposite, it *spreads human beings (or animals) out in an open*, undefined, non-communicating space."

Deleuze, Gilles; Guattari, Félix, *Mille plateaux: capitalisme et schizophrénie*, Les Éditions de Minuit, Paris, 1980; (English version: *A Thousand Plateaus: Capitalism and Schizophrenia*, Athlone Press, London, 1987).

Errare Humanum Est...

Cain, Abel, and Architecture

The primordial separation of humanity into nomads and settlers results in two different ways of living in the world and therefore of thinking about space. It is widely believed that the settlers—as the inhabitants of the city—can be considered the 'architects' of the world, while the nomads—as the inhabitants of the deserts and the open spaces—should be seen as 'anti-architects,' experimental adventurers, and therefore against architecture and, more generally, the transformation of the landscape.[1] But perhaps things are a little more complex. If we look back on the story of Cain and Abel in architectural terms, we can observe how the relation nomadism and settlement establish with the construction of symbolic space springs from an original ambiguity. As we read in *Genesis,* the first sexual division of humanity—Adam and Eve—is followed, in the second generation, by a division of labor and therefore of space. The sons of Adam and Eve embody the two souls in which the human race is divided from the outset: Cain is the sedentary soul, Abel the nomadic one. In keeping with God's will, Cain devoted his time to agriculture, Abel to sheep rearing. Adam and Eve thus left their sons an equal legacy, dividing the world in two: Cain was the owner of all the land, Abel the owner of all the living beings.

But the parents, ingenuously relying on brotherly love, didn't think about the fact that all living things need land to move and to live, and above all, that shepherds need pastures for their flocks. Thus it happened that in the wake of an argument Cain accused Abel of trespassing and—as we all know—killed him, condemning himself to a destiny of eternal wandering as punishment for his fratricidal sin: "When thou tillest the ground, it shall not henceforth yield unto thee her strength; a fugitive and a vagabond shalt thou be in the earth."[2] According to the etymological roots of the names of the two brothers, Cain can be identified with *Homo Faber,* the man who works and tames nature to materially construct a new artificial universe, while Abel, whose job was, all told, less tiring and more amusing, can be seen as that *Homo Ludens* so dear to the Situationists, the man who plays and constructs an ephemeral system of relations between nature and life. Their different use of space also implies a different *use of time* derived from the original division of labor. The work of Abel, which consists in *going* to fields to feed his animals, is one of privilege with respect to the labors of Cain, who has to *stay* in the fields to plough, sow and reap the fruits of the earth. While most of Cain's time is spent on *work,* and is therefore entirely a useful, productive time, Abel has a great quantity of free time to devote to intellectual speculation, exploration of the earth, adventure and, therefore, to play, the non-utilitarian time *par excellence.* This free and therefore *playful* time leads Abel to experiment and to construct an initial symbolic universe around him. The activity of walking through the landscape to watch the flocks leads to the first mapping of space and to that attribution of symbolic and aesthetic values to the territory that was to lead to the birth of landscape architecture. So from the very beginning artistic creation, as well as that rejection of work and therefore of the *opus* that was to develop with the Parisian Dadaists and Surrealists, a sort of recreational-contemplative sloth that lies at the base of the anti-artistic *flânerie* that crosses the 20th century, was associated with walking.

Walkscapes — walking as an aesthetic practice

Cain and Abel

"The names of the brothers are a matched pair of opposites. 'Abel' comes from the Hebrew *hebel* meaning 'breath' or 'vapor': anything that lives and moves and is transient, including his own life. The root of 'Cain' appears to be the verb *kanah*: to 'acquire', 'get', 'own property', and so 'rule' or "subjugate". 'Cain' also means 'metal-smith'. And since, in several languages—even Chinese—the words for 'violence' and 'subjugation' are linked to the discovery of metal, it is perhaps the destiny of Cain and his descendants to practice the black arts of technology."

BRUCE CHATWIN, *The Songlines*, Viking, New York, 1987.

Homo Ludens

"In the course of time we have come to realize that we are not so reasonable after all as the eighteen century, with its worship of reason and its naïve optimism, thought us; hence modern fashion tends to designate our species *Homo Sapiens*, as *Homo Faber*: Man the Maker. But though faber may not be quite so dubious as sapiens, it is, as a name specific of the human being, even less appropriate, seeing that many animals, too, are makers. There is a third function, however, applicable to both human and animal life, and just as important as reasoning and making—namely, playing. It seems to me that next to *Homo Faber*, and perhaps on the same level as *Homo Sapiens, Homo Ludens*, Man the Player, deserves a place in our nomenclature."

JOHAN HUIZINGA, *Homo Ludens; Versuch einer Bestimmung des Spielelementes der Kultur*, Pantheon, Amsterdam-Leipzig, 1939 (English version: *Homo Ludens: A Study of The Play Element in Culture*, Routledge & Kegan Paul, London, 1949).

But it is interesting to note that after the murder Cain is punished by God by being condemned to roam the face of the earth: Abel's nomadism is transformed from a condition of privilege to one of divine punishment. The *error* of fratricide is punished with a sentence to *err* without a home, eternally lost in the land of Nod, the infinite desert where Abel had previously roamed. And it should be emphasized that after the death of Abel the first cities are constructed by the descendants of Cain: Cain, the farmer condemned to wander, gives rise to the sedentary life and therefore to another sin, he carries with him the origins of the stationary life of the farmer and those of the nomadic life of Abel, both experienced as a punishment and an error. But actually, according to *Genesis,* it is Jabal, a direct descendent of Cain, "the father of such as dwell in tents, and of such as have cattle."[3] The nomads come from the lineage of Cain, who was a settler forced to become a nomad, and they carry the wanderings of Abel in their roots (also etymologically).

Bruce Chatwin reminds us that "no people but the Jews have ever felt more keenly the moral ambiguities of settlement. Their God is a projection of their perplexity. [...] Yahwèh, in origin, is a God of the Way. His sanctuary is the Mobile Ark, His House a tent, His Altar a cairn of rough stones. And though He may promise His Children a well-watered land [...] He secretly desires for them the Desert."[4] And Richard Sennet continues, stating that in reality "Yahwèh was a God of Time rather than of Place, a God who promises to give his followers a divine sense of their mournful wanderings."[5] This uncertainty about architecture dates back to the dawn of humanity. The two great families into which the human race is divided have two different spatial experiences: that of the cave and the plough, excavating space from the body of the earth, and that of the tent that moves across the earth's surface without leaving any lasting traces. These two ways of dwelling on the Earth correspond to two conceptions of architecture itself: an architecture seen as physical construction of space and form, as opposed to an architecture seen as perception and symbolic construction of space. Observing the origins of architecture through the nomad-settler polarity, it would appear that the art of constructing space—or what we normally call 'architecture'—was originally an invention of the settlers which evolved from the construction of the first rural villages to

Walkscapes — walking as an aesthetic practice

that of the cities and the great temples. The commonly held belief is that architecture was born of the necessity for a 'space of staying,' as opposed to nomadism, understood as a 'space of going.'

Actually, the relationship between architecture and nomadism cannot be directly expressed as an opposition of "architecture or nomadism." There is a much more profound relation that connects architecture to nomadism through the notion of the journey or path. In fact it is probable that it was nomadism, or more precisely 'wandering,' that gave rise to architecture, revealing the need for a symbolic construction of the landscape. All this began well before the appearance of the concept of nomadism itself, during the intercontinental roving of the first men of the Paleolithic period, many millennia before the construction of the temples and the cities.

Nomadic Space and "Erratic" Space

The division of labor between Cain and Abel produced two distinct but not fully self-sufficient civilizations. The nomad, in fact, lives in contrast but also in osmosis with the settler: farmers and shepherds need to continuously trade their products and require a *hybrid,* or more precisely *neutral,* space in which this trade is possible. The Sahel has precisely this function: it is the *edge* of the desert where nomadic sheep-rearing and sedentary agriculture mingle, forming an unstable buffer zone between the settled city and the nomadic city, the full and the empty.[6] Gilles Deleuze and Félix Guattari have described these two different spatial concepts with a very clear image: "The sedentary space is *striated* by walls, enclosures and routes between the enclosures, while the nomadic space is *smooth,* marked only by 'strokes' that are erased or shift with the journey."[7]

In other words sedentary space is denser, more solid, and therefore *full,* while that of the nomad is less dense, more fluid, and therefore *empty.* The nomadic space is an infinite, uninhabited, often impervious void: a desert in which orientation is difficult, as in an immense sea where the only recognizable feature is the track left by walking, a mobile, evanescent sign. The nomadic city is the path itself, the most

Steps of *Australopithecus*, Laetoli, Tanzania The oldest evidence of the existence of man are the traces of a walk that took place 3,700,000 years ago, solidified in volcanic mud. The footprints, discovered at the end of the 1970s by Mary Leakey, were left there by an adult *Australopithecus Afarensis* and his son, who both walked in an erect position. The study of the joints of these two walkers shows that they were equally capable of climbing trees.

JEAN GUILAINE, *La Préhistoire d'un continent à l'autre*, Librairie Larousse, Paris, 1989.

stable sign in the void, and the form of this city is the sinuous line drawn by the succession of points in motion. The points of departure and arrival are less important, while the space between is the *space of going,* the very essence of nomadism, the place in which to celebrate the everyday ritual of *eternal wandering.* Just as the sedentary path structures and gives life to the city, in nomadism the path becomes the symbolic place of the life of the community.

The nomadic city is not the trail of a past left as a tracing on the ground, it is the present that occupies, again and again, those segments of the territory on which the journey takes place, that part of the landscape walked, perceived, and experienced in the *hic et nunc* of the transhumance. It is from this vantage point that the territory can be interpreted, memorized, and mapped in its becoming. Lacking stable reference points, the nomad has developed the capacity to construct his own map for every occasion, whose geography is in constant change, deformed in time due to the movements of the observer and the perpetual transformation of the territory. The nomadic map is a void where the paths connect wells, oases, holy places, good pastures and spaces that change rapidly. It is a map that seems to reflect a *liquid* space in which the full fragments of the space of *staying* float in the void of going, in which always shifting paths remain visible only until they are erased by the wind. The nomadic space is furrowed by vectors, by unstable arrows that constitute temporary links rather than defined roads: the same system of representation of space found in the plan of a Paleolithic village carved in stone in the Val Camonica, in the maps of the "walkabouts" of the Australian Aborigines, and in the *psychogeographic* maps of the Situationists.

While in the settler's eyes nomadic spaces are empty, for nomads these voids are full of invisible traces: every little dissimilarity is an event, a useful landmark for the construction of a mental map composed of points (particular places), lines (paths), and surfaces (homogeneous territories) that are transformed over time.

The ability to *know how* to see in the void of places and therefore to *know how to name* these places was learned in the millennia preceding the birth of nomadism. The perception/construction of space begins with the wanderings of man in the Paleolithic landscape. While initial-

Sahel "The word 'Sahara' comes from *sahra,* meaning an empty space 'without pasture', while 'Sahel', the southern edge of the Sahara, comes from the Arabic *sahel* and means 'shore' or 'border'. The Sahel is the margin of great empty space across which, like a great sea, one 'berths' at something stable and marked by the presence of man. The Sahel, therefore, is the place where nomadic sheepherding and sedentary agriculture mingle, a mutable border that forms the place of trade and continuous rebalancing between the two civilizations."

EUGENIO TURRI, *Gli uomini delle tende,* Comunità, Milan, 1983.

Terrain Vague "An empty place without cultivation or construction, in a city or a suburb, an indeterminate space without precise boundaries. It is an apparently forgotten place where the memory of the past seems to predominate over the present, an obsolete place where certain values remain in spite of a complete abandonment of the rest of urban activity, a place that is definitively exogenous and extraneous, outside the circuit of the productive structures of the city, an internal, uninhabited, unproductive and often dangerous island, simultaneously on the margins of the urban system and a fundamental part of the system [...] In the end it looks like the counter-image of the city, both in the sense of a critique and of a clue for a possible way to go beyond. [...] The relationship between the absence of utilization and the sentiment of freedom is fundamental to grasp all the evocative, paradoxical power of the *terrain vague* in the perception of the contemporary city. The void is absence, but it is also hope, the space of the possible. The indefinite and uncertain is also the absence of limits, an almost oceanic sensation, to use one of Freud's terms, the expectation of mobility and wandering. [...] The presence of power invites escape from its all-pervasive enterprise, sedentary comfort invites unprotected nomadism, urban order invites the indefinite nature of the *terrain vague,* the true index of the aesthetic and ethical questions raised by the issues of contemporary society."

IGNASI DE SOLÀ-MORALES, "Urbanité Intersticielle", in *Inter Art Actuel,* 61, Quebec, 1995.

Journey, Experience, Danger, Path "Behind the voyage there is often a desire for existential change. Travel is atonement for a sin, initiation, cultural growth, experience: "The Indo-European root of the word 'experience' is *per,* which has been interpreted as 'to attempt', 'to test', 'to risk', connotations that survive in the word 'peril'. The oldest connotations of trial of *per* appear in the Latin terms for experience: *experior, experimentum.* This conception of experience as a test, as a passage through a form of action that measures the true dimensions and nature of the person or the object that undergoes it, also describes the most ancient conception of the effects of the voyage on the traveler. Many of the secondary meanings of *per* explicitly refer to motion: 'to cross a space', 'to reach a goal', 'to go outside'. The implication of risk present in 'peril' is evident in the gothic kin of *per* (in which the P becomes F): ferm, fare, fear, ferry. One of the German words for experience, *Erfahrung,* comes from Old German, irfaran: 'to travel', to go out, to cross or to wander. The deeply rooted idea that the voyage is an experience that tests and perfects the character of the traveler is clear in the German adjective *bewandert,* which today means 'wise', 'expert' or 'versed,' but which originally (in the texts of the 15th century) simply was applied to someone who had 'traveled much'."

ERICH J. LEED, *The Mind of the Traveler. From Gilgamesh to Global Tourism,* Basic Books, New York, 1991.

ly men could have used the tracks created by the seasonal migrations of animals through the vegetation, it is probable that from a certain period onward they began to blaze their own trails, to learn to orient themselves using geographical reference points, and to leave increasingly stable recognizable signs on the landscape. The history of the origins of man is a history of walking, of migrations of peoples and cultural and religious exchanges that took place along intercontinental trajectories. The slow, complex operation of appropriation and mapping of the territory was the result of the incessant walking of the first humans.

The 'walkabout' is the system of routes with which the indigenous peoples of Australia have mapped the entire continent. Every mountain, river and spring belongs to a complex system of path-stories—*the songlines*—that continuously interweave to form a single "history of the Dream Time," the story of the origins of mankind. Each of these paths is connected to a song, and each song is connected to one or more mythological tales set in the territory. The entire culture of the Australian aborigines—passed down from generation to generation thanks to a still-active oral tradition—is based on a complex mythological epic of stories and geographies that exist in the same space. Each path has its own song and the complex of the songlines constitutes a network of erratic, symbolic paths that cross and describe the space, like a sort of chanted guidebook. It is as if Time and History were updated again and again by 'walking them,' re-crossing the places and the myths associated with them in a musical deambulation that is simultaneously religious and geographic.[8]

This type of journey, still visible in Aboriginal cultures, belongs to a phase of human history preceding that of nomadism. We can define this type of path as 'erratic.' It is important, in fact, to make a distinction between the concepts of roaming (*errare*) and nomadism. While the nomadic journey is linked to cyclical movements of livestock during the transhumance, erratic movement is connected to the pursuit of prey of the hunter-gatherers of the Paleolithic era. In general, it is not correct to speak of nomadism before the Neolithic revolution in the seventh millennium BC, because nomadism and settlement are both the result of the new productive utilization of the land that began with the climate change following the last glacial period.

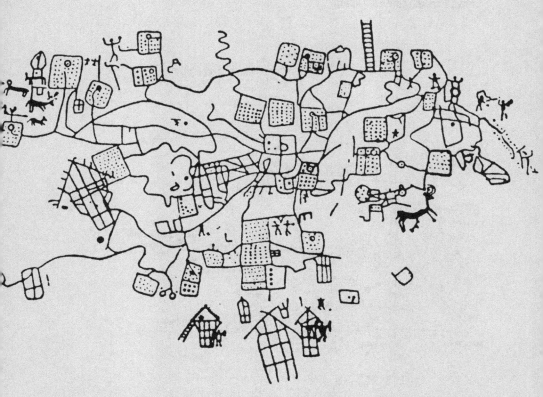

Map "One of the first maps representing a system of routes dates back to about 10,000 years ago, and is engraved on a stone in the Val Camonica in northern Italy, in a grouping of about 130,000 incisions made between the heights of 400 and 1000 meters above sea level. This is an image that represents the system of connections of the everyday life of a Paleolithic village. The map, rather than deciphering the objects, represents the dynamic of a complex system in which the lines of the routes in the void intertwine to provide access for the different full elements of the territory. We can recognize scenes of men in activity, paths, steps, huts, pile-dwellings, bordered fields and zones for livestock."

MARIANO PALLOTTINI, *Alle origini della città europea*, Quasar, Rome, 1985.

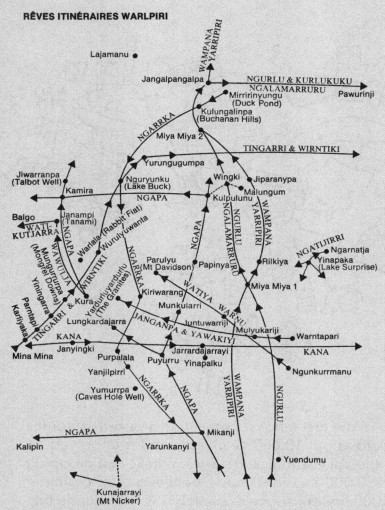

Songlines in the region of the Warlpiri language, Australia, 2000 AD The walkabout of the Australian aborigines is a complex of sung itineraries that retrace places and the myths connected with them, as in a sacred dance through their own space and their own origins. In the map drawn by Patrick Mérienne some meanings of the terms are: *Ngapa*=rain; Waitya-warnu=seeds; *Ngarrka*=initiated man; *Wawulja*=invincible; *Yarripiri*=serpent; *Janganapa & Yawankiyi*=opossum & black plum; *Ngatijirri*=green parrot.

BARBARA GLOWCZEWSKI, *YAPA peintres aborigènes,* Baudoin Lebon, Paris, 1991.

Walkabout "The mud fell from their thighs, like placenta from a baby. Then, like the baby's first cry, each Ancestor opened his mouth and called out, 'I AM!' [...] And this first 'I am!', this primordial act of naming, was held, then and forever after, as the most sacred and secret couplet of the Ancestor's song.

Each of the Ancients [...] put his left foot forward and called out a second name. He put his right foot forward and called out a third name. He named the waterhole, the reed beds, the gum trees—calling to right and left, calling all things into being and weaving their names into verses.

The Ancients sang their way all over the world. They sang the rivers and ranges, salt-pans and sand dunes. [...] wherever their tracks led they left a trail of music.

They wrapped the whole world in a web of song; and at last, when the Earth was sung, they felt tired. [...] Some sank into the ground where they stood. Some crawled into caves. Some crept away to their 'Eternal Homes', to the ancestral waterholes that bore them.

All of them went 'back in'."

BRUCE CHATWIN, *The Songlines*, Viking, New York, 1987.

Way "The village is the place to which the roads tend, a sort of expansion of the highway as a lake of a river. [...] The word is from the Latin *villa,* which together with *via,* a way, or more anciently *ved* and *vella,* Varro derives from *veho* to carry, because the villa is the place to and from which things are carried. They who got their living by teaming were said *vellaturam facere.* Hence too apparently the Latin word *vilis* and our 'vile'; also 'villain'. This suggests what kind of degeneracy villagers are liable to. They are way-worn by the travel that goes by and over them, without travelling themselves."

HENRY D. THOREAU, *Walking* (1862), Applewood Books, Boston, 1987.

Getting Lost "Getting lost means that between us and space there is not only a relationship of dominion, of control on the part of the subject, but also the possibility that space can dominate us. There are moments in life in which we learn how to learn from the space around us. [...] We are no longer capable of giving a value, a meaning to the possibility of getting lost. To change places, to come to terms with different worlds, to be forced to continuously recreate our points of reference, is regenerating at a psychic level, but today no one would recommend such an experience. In primitive cultures, on the other hand, if someone never gets lost he never grows up. And this is done in the desert, the forest, places that are a sort of machine through which to attain other states of consciousness."

FRANCO LA CECLA, *Perdersi, l'uomo senza ambiente,* Laterza, Bari, 1988.

Nomadism takes place in vast empty spaces, but spaces that are familiar, and a return trip is planned; wandering, on the other hand, happens in an empty space that has not yet been mapped, without any defined destination. In a certain sense the path of the nomad is a cultural evolution of wandering, a sort of 'specialization.' It is important to remember that agriculture and livestock-raising are two activities derived from the specialization of the two primitive productive activities—gathering and hunting—, both of which required wandering. These two activities, which consisted in obtaining food by roaming the land, evolved over time thanks to the gradual taming of animals (sheep-rearing) and of plants (agriculture), and only after many millennia did they begin to generate sedentary space and nomadic space. Therefore both the routes of the sedentary world and the journeys of the nomad are derived from the erratic, Paleolithic path. The notion of path belongs simultaneously to both cultures, i.e. to the builders of 'settled cities' and to those of 'errant cities.'

Space before the Neolithic era was utterly free of those signs that began to mark the surface of the Earth with the advent of agriculture and settlement. The only architecture in the Paleolithic world was the path, the first anthropic sign capable of imposing an artificial order on the territories of natural chaos. Space, which for primitive man was empathic—experienced as being animated with magical presences— began to include the first elements of order in the Paleolithic period. What seemed like an irrational, random space based on concrete material experience slowly began to transform into rational and geometric space generated by the abstraction of thought. This was a passage from a mere utilitarian use for the finding of nourishment to an attribution of mystical and sacred meanings to physical space. A passage from a *quantitative* to a *qualitative* space, filling the surrounding void with a certain number of *full places* that served for orientation. In this way the multidirectional space of natural chaos began to be transformed into a space ordered, in keeping with the two main directions clearly visible in the void: the direction of the sun and that of the horizon.

At the end of the Paleolithic era, therefore, the landscape deciphered by man probably resembled that of the walkabout: a space constructed by vectors of erratic pathways, by a series of geographical features connected to mythical events and assembled in sequence, and it was probably ordered in keeping with the fixed directions of the vertical and the horizontal: the sun and the horizon.

Walking, though it is not the physical construction of a space, implies a transformation of the place and its meanings. The mere physical presence of man in an unmapped space and the variations of perceptions he receives crossing it, constitute a form of transformation of the landscape that, without leaving visible signs, culturally modifies the meaning of space and therefore the space itself. Before the Neolithic era, and thus before the menhirs, the only symbolic architecture capable of modifying the environment was walking, an action that is simultaneously an act of perception and creativity, of reading and writing the territory.

From the Path to the Menhir

The first *situated object* in the human landscape springs directly from the universe of roaming and nomadism. While the horizon is a stable, more or less straight line depending upon the landscape itself, the sun has a less definite movement, following a trajectory that appears clearly vertical only in its two moments of vicinity to the horizon: sunrise and sunset. The desire to stabilize the vertical dimension was probably one of the motivations behind the creation of the first artificial element in space: the menhir.

Menhirs appear for the first time in the Neolithic age and represent the simplest objects, but with the greatest density of meaning, of the entire Stone Age. Their raising is the first human act of physical transformation of the landscape: a large stone lying horizontally on the ground is still just a stone without symbolic connotations, but when it is raised vertically and planted in the ground it is transformed into a new presence that stops time and space: it institutes a 'time zero' that extends into eternity, and a new system of relations with the elements of the surrounding landscape.

An invention of such scope could satisfy many different aims, and this partially explains the great number of different interpretations

Walkscapes — walking as an aesthetic practice

that have been made of the menhirs. It is probable, in fact, that many menhirs had multiple, simultaneous functions: it is almost certain that, in general, they were connected to the cult of fertility, of the mother goddess Earth and the worship of the Sun, but the same stones probably also indicated the places where legendary heroes had died, sacred sites of potent chthonic energy, places where water was found (another sacred element), or boundaries and property lines. What interests us about the megaliths is not so much the study of the cults involved as the relationship established by the stones with the territory: *where* they were placed. We can approach this question by considering the name still used today for the menhirs by the shepherds of Laconi, in Sardinia: *perdas litteradas* or 'lettered stones,' 'stones of letters.'[9] This reference to writing can, in fact, explain at least three different uses of the monoliths: surfaces on which to inscribe symbolic figures, elements with which to write on the territory, and signals with which to describe the territory. The first interpretation of the term *litteradas* simply refers to the fact that on the main face of some of the stones different symbols are placed, as on the Egyptian obelisks. The second indicates that these stones were used to architecturally construct the landscape as a sort of *geometry*—seen in the etymological sense of 'measurement of the earth'—with which to design abstract figures to oppose natural chaos: the point (the isolated menhir); the line (the rhythmical alignment of multiple stones); the surface (the *cromlech,* or the portion of space enclosed by menhirs placed in a circle). The third interpretation indicates that the stones, beyond *geometry,* also revealed the *geography* of the place, serving to describe its physical structure and its productive and/or mystical-religious utilization. In other words, they were signals placed along the major routes of crossing.

It has been noted that often the zones of megalithic activity in the Neolithic era coincide with those of the development of hunting in the Paleolithic period. This prompts reflection on the link between the menhirs and the paths of Paleolithic roaming and those of nomadic transhumance. In effect it is hard to imagine how the travelers of antiquity could have crossed entire continents without the help of maps, roads and signs. Yet an incredible traffic of travelers and merchants continuously crossed nearly impassable forests and uncharted territories, apparently without excessive difficulty. It is very probable that the menhirs functioned as a system of territorial orientation, easily deciphered by those who understood its language: a sort of guide sculpted in the landscape, leading the traveler to his destination from one signal to another along the intercontinental routes.

The menhirs had a relationship with the routes of commerce, which was often driven by activities of livestock-rearing. For the Romans the menhirs were simply simulacra of Mercury, or the natural predecessors of the *Hermae* that guarded the *quadrivium,* the crossroads symbolizing the four directions of the world, where man encountered different possibilities for the future, where Oedipus ran up against his incestuous fate, where it was best, therefore, to seek the protection of a god. Hermes or Mercury, the messenger of the gods, was the god of wayfarers and of commerce (*mercari* = to trade), of thieves and profit, and the protector of the roads and intersections, in the dual sense of earthly roads and those of the soul to the afterworld.[10]

Even today, in Puglia, in the south of Italy, certain menhirs stand along the boundaries separating different territories, places which were probably the sites of clashes or encounters between different villages in ancient times. This hypothesis is supported by the fact that the raising of such monoliths required the work of an enormous number of men, and therefore the inhabitants of more than one village had to be involved. Malagrinò cites the example of the largest monolith of Carnac, the menhir Locmariaquer, 23 meters high, weighing 300 tons, whose erection is calculated as requiring the force of at least 3,000 people. If such a large number of people did not come from a concerted effort of different populations, we would have to posit the existence of a village so large as to be a veritable megalopolis for the time. The impossibility of the existence of such large tribes leads to the hypothesis that the menhirs were not positioned in territory belonging to one particular village, but in 'neutral' zones with which multiple populations could identify, a fact which would also explain the use, on a single site, of stones from different regions, some of which were even hundreds of kilometers distant from the site.[11]

The zones in which the megalithic works were built were, therefore, either a sort of sanctuary utilized by the surrounding pop-

Walkscapes — walking as an aesthetic practice

Menhir The word *menhir* comes from the Breton dialect and literally means 'long stone' (men = stone, and hir = long). The erection of the menhirs represents the first physical transformation of the landscape from a natural to an artificial state. The menhir is the new presence in the space of the Neolithic period, it is the simultaneously abstract and living object from which architecture (the tripartite column) and sculpture (the stele-statue) were later to develop.
ROBERT FLEMMING HAIZER, *L'età dei giganti*, Marsilio, Venice, 1990

Menhir Sa Perda Iddocca, Laconi, Sardinia, IV millenium b. C.

Menhir Genna Arrele I, Laconi, Sardinia, IV millenium b. C.

Perdas Litteradas "Lettered stones" is the name given to menhirs in Sardinia, in the territory of Laconi. I was informed of this directly by Antonia Manca di Villermosa, a scholar of Sardinian megaliths, who discovered the first Sardinian menhir, Genna Arrele I. "Donna Antonia", as she was called by the inhabitants of the town, studied the menhirs in the territory of Laconi for many years, through the legends and songs that still survive in the oral tradition. Thanks to her determination a Civic Archaeological Museum has been opened at Laconi of the statue-menhirs, with displays of forty monoliths from the surrounding areas.

Dancing stones Among the many names given to menhirs in different cultures, there is also the term "dancing stones", probably due to the human dimension of the stones that expressed a living presence inside the object, but perhaps also due to the ritual dances and processions that took place around them. "These stones planted in the ground are alive—say the Irish peasants and shepherds—they turn, dance, bow, drink, and are called *fear breagach*='the false man', 'the fake man' in Gaelic. […] There is a particular insistence on the dance; today the menhir are stones, 'false' or 'fake' men, but once upon a time they were real men: God punished them, turning them into stone—but living stones—because he caught them in the act of dancing a profane, sinful dance."

FULVIO JESI, *Il linguaggio delle pietre*, Rizzoli, Milan, 1978.

Genna Arrele I, Laconi, Sardinia, 4th millennium BC This is the first Sardinian menhir, discovered in 1957, and on display today at the National Archaeological Museum in Sassari. The figure at the top, interpreted as the arch of an eyebrow, could also be interpreted as the imprint of *benou,* the sunbeam; the central figure, interpreted as an overturned man, could be interpreted as the symbol of the *ka,* of eternal wandering in adoration of the sun; the figure below, interpreted as a vulva or a double dagger, could be interpreted as an arrow. The plain of Genna Arrele, where the menhir was found, is on the route of transhumance leading to Valle Iddocca. "It is not rare for the dense stones to be found in the proximity or right on the edge of ancient routes that are traveled even today, especially in the transhumance routes of the shepherds, or in the forks of trees. A sheep track thousands of years old passes between two alignments of dense monumental stones, which act as a *propylaeum,* on the Perda Iddocca-Làconi pass. It is plausible that the menhirs were created and erected not only for their local function of simulacra of worship on the part of the inhabitants of the villages in the area, but also as points of reference, signals or stopping places for wayfarers; in other words, they had a purpose of general and, I would say, public interest, and yet, as in the silent, arcane space occupied by the menhirs in a row of Perda Iddocca, human groups did not linger around them for sacred ceremonies of pastoral transhumance."

GIOVANNI LILLIU, *La civiltà dei sardi, dal paleolitico all'età dei nuraghi,* Nuova ERI, Turin, 1988.

ulations for festivities, or more probably stopping places along the main routes of transit, places with the function of today's highway rest stops. These places were visited throughout the year—and especially during the period of transhumance—by a great multitude of different people. Along the way the menhirs attracted the attention of the wayfarer to communicate the presence of singular facts and information regarding the surrounding territory, information useful for the continuation of the journey, such as changes of direction, points of passage, intersections, passes, dangers. But perhaps the menhirs also indicated places where ritual celebrations were held, connected to wandering: sacred paths, initiations, processions, games, contests, dances, theatrical and musical performances. The entire voyage, which had been the place of events, stories, and myths around or along the menhirs, encountered a space for representation of itself: tales of travels and legends were celebrated and ritualized around the stones planted in the ground. Therefore the journey-path created, through the menhirs, a new type of space, a space *around,* which the Egyptians later were able to transform into a space *inside.* The menhirs were positioned in relation to the road structure, but in contrast to what one might expect, they did not function as perspective poles—they were placed laterally with respect to the path. In the case of multiple menhirs lined up in a row, besides defining a direction, they separated two spaces, or more precisely they architecturally constructed the border of a space to be crossed or perhaps danced in, a rhythmical space, geometrically defined, that represents the first architecture, in the sense of physical construction of a complex symbolic space, a 'space of going' and therefore not a 'space of staying:' the same type of space that was to be constructed in the first Egyptian works of architecture.

While in the world of the villages and the cultivated fields the erratic path had been transformed into a trail and then a road, giving rise to the architecture of the city, in the empty spaces of the nomadic universe the path conserves its symbolic elements of Paleolithic roaming and transfers them into the sacred spaces of the Egyptian temples. From this moment on it would be increasingly difficult to separate architecture from the path.

The *Benben* and the *Ka*

The Egyptian civilization is a stationary one, but still closely linked to its nomadic origins, conserving a substantial continuity with the Paleolithic cultures in its symbolic and religious expressions. The menhir and the path, the architectural archetypes of the earlier ages, are transformed by the Egyptian civilization into the first true works of architecture, the former as *volume* and the latter as *interior space.*

According to Sigfried Giedion, the birth of the first volume in space was represented in Egyptian culture by the myth of the *benben,* "the first stone to emerge from the chaos," a monolith said to represent the vertical petrifaction of the first sunbeam, thus connected to the symbolism of the menhirs, the obelisks, and the pyramids. The birth of interior space, on the other hand, is connected to the concept of the *ka,* the symbol of *eternal wandering,* a sort of divine spirit that symbolized movement, life, energy and embodies the memory of the perilous migrations of the Paleolithic period. The symbol of the *benben* is a conical monolith with a luminous tip, while the hieroglyphic for *ka* is composed of two arms raised skyward, probably representing the act of transmission of divine energy and of worship of the Sun. The two symbols would seem to be present in the menhirs placed along the routes of transhumance in Sardinia, at whose top a sign is sculpted that could be interpreted as a sunbeam, with a large figure at the center that is very similar to the symbol of *ka* with its raised arms. *Ka* is one of man's most ancient symbols, and because it is frequently found in many different civilizations at great distances from one another, we could suppose that it was comprehensible for the multitudes of people who crossed the continents on foot: a symbol understood by all the errant populations of the Paleolithic period.

Giedion states that the "organization of the large temples of the New Kingdom expressed the idea of eternal wandering," and that the first works of architecture in stone were the result of the wanderings of the *ka.* One of the most spectacular Egyptian constructions is the great hypostyle of Karnak, a passage inside enormous rows of parallel columns that reminds us (not only for the uncanny name resemblance, containing the root 'ka') of the spatial rhythm of Carnac, the largest alignment of menhirs in the world, probably utilized for sacred dances and ritual processions.[12] Thus there would appear to be a continuity between the sacred paths flanked by rows of megaliths and the first Egyptian hypostyle architecture flanked by columns. In the Egyptian temples, with the *cella obscura* which contained the image of the god, each part of the complex was conceived as a place of transit. The large hypostyles with their forest of columns served as a passageway for the king and for the procession that took the god from one sanctuary to another. There were no spaces designed to contain a congregation attending a religious function, but there were spaces to walk through, built for the initiations that made the eternal wandering sacred and symbolic.[13]

Before the physical transformation of the face of the Earth that began with the menhirs, the territory had undergone a cultural transformation based on walking, an action that took place only on the surface of the planet, without penetrating it. The space of the path, therefore, precedes architectonic space; it is an immaterial space with symbolic-religious meanings. For thousands of years, when the physical construction of a symbolic place was still unthinkable, the crossing of space represented an aesthetic means through which it was possible to inhabit the world. Religion, dance, music, and narrative in its epic forms of geographical description and initiation of entire peoples were associated with wandering. The path/story was transformed into a literary genre connected to the voyage, the description and representation of space. The attempts to go 'beyond art,' referred to in the next chapter, have utilized the path to undermine the forms of traditional representation and to arrive at action constructed in real space.

Up to this point we have seen that the problem of the birth of architecture, be it as a principle of structuring the landscape, or as the architecture of interior space, is connected to the erratic path and its nomadic evolution.

Once this important point has been clarified, and thus once we have refuted the erroneous but common conviction that architecture is an invention of the sedentary, settled world rather than the nomadic world, we will not plunge into the subsequent history of architecture, but stop here at the phase of wandering, of the path seen as symbolic

Walkscapes — walking as an aesthetic practice

action rather than as a sign or object in space. What follows is a sort of history of the city-as-path, from the first forms of the Dada readymade to the experiences of the 1960s. The aesthetic practice of walking has freed itself, in the last century, from all religious ritual connotations to assume the increasingly evident appearance of an independent art form. In order for this secularization of the practice of walking and its return to the purely aesthetic sphere to take place, it was necessary to wait for the avant-gardes of the 20th century, when Dada made the first lay pilgrimage to a Christian church.

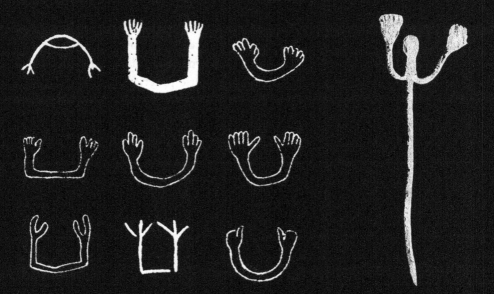

Left, the hieroglyphics of the ka in different cultures; right, "man with raised arms", Bandiagara, Mali.

The *ka*, the spirit of eternal wandering The Egyptian concept of the *ka*, which symbolized "eternal wandering", movement, vital force, carries with it the memory of the infinite and perilous paleolithic migrations. The hieroglyphic of the *ka* is composed of two raised arms, indicating how divine energy is transmitted from the god as is by direct infusion from above, or through the protective embrace whose symbol is a sort of upside-down *ka*. The symbol of the *ka*, with the hands of disproportionate size, is connected to the gesture of sun worship which dates back to prehistoric times in many civilizations, from Africa to Scandinavia.

"There is a bridge to the religious concepts of primeval times where one would last except it. This is the notion of the *ka*, which was further elaborated by the Heliopolitan theologians and incorporated into their religious system [...] The beginning of stone architecture is separably bound up with the concept of the *ka*, and it was for the *ka* of the founder of the Third Dinasty, King Zoser, that stone architecture first came into being".

SIEGFRIED GIEDION, *The Eternal Present. A Contribution on Constancy and Change*, Pantheon Books, New York, 1964.

Benben and **Benou** The *Benben* stone, venerated in the temples of Heliopolis, is a monolith with a conical form and a crested bird at its summit, the *Benou*. The etymological root of the two names is *bn* or *wbn*="light", "brightness", "ascent". The *Benben* is the first apparition of the Sun God (Atum-Ra) after the primordial chaos, it is "the stone that first emerged from the chaos": the petrifaction of the first ray of the sun at dawn that was transformed, with geometric abstraction, into the obelisk with a luminous point and later into the pyramid, the very image of the Sun that rises and the place of union between heaven and earth. *Benou* is the symbol of immortality and resurrection, it is the blue heron that was first to alight on the original hill that emerged from the mud—the *Benben*—over which the Sun had risen for the first time from the horizon, and where Atum-Ra had created the first couple of the human race.

On the relationship between *Benou* and *Benben* cf. SERGE SAUNERON & JEAN YOYOTTE, "La Naissance du monde", in *Sources Orientales,* vol. I, Paris, 1959.

Alignment of Carnac, Brittany, 7th millennium, BC This is the largest alignment of menhirs in the world, a sort of enormous open-air temple, probably used as a place of sacred processions and rituals connected to the rite of eternal wandering and sun worship. Due to its particular astronomical orientations it has been defined as a huge stone calendar. This was a place in which the different communities that crossed the region met periodically, with visitors on a national or perhaps international scale. There are 3,000 megaliths (originally almost 15,000), of progressively decreasing height, arranged in parallel rows. The system, with an overall length of 4,000 meters, is divided into three groups of alignments in succession: Ménec, Kermario, Kerlescan.

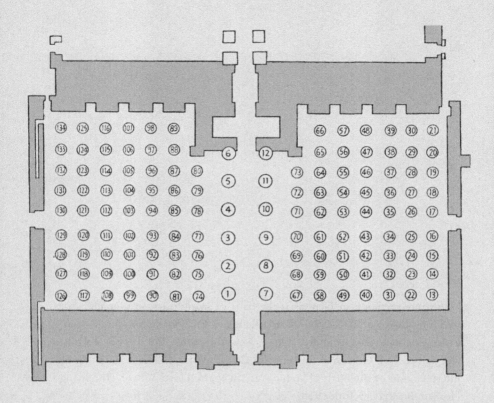

Temple of Amon in Karnak, Egypt, 2nd millennium, BC
The space of the journey materializes for the first time in an interior architectural space in the temple hall of the temple built by Ramses II in the first half of the second millennium, BC. Formed by 134 columns arranged in 16 rows in the east-west direction, it is a passage between the parallels that recall (not just for the name that contains the root ka) the alignments of the great Carnac complex. Sigfried Giedion considers it "the most importent contribution of Egypt to the history of architecture ... It is not a gathering place for a covenant of devotees; nor a place of rest; it is simply a passing passage, the most colossal ever conceived."

Sigfried Giedion, *The Eternal Present*, 1964

Notes

[1] This interpretation of Genesis is the basis of many texts on nomadic space, we find it in: Eugenio Turri, Gli uomini delle tende, Edizioni Comunità, Milano 1983; Bruce Chatwin, The Songlines, Viking, New York 1987; Eric J. Leed, La mente del viaggiatore. Dall'Odissea al turismo globale, Il mulino, Bologna 1992. See also the interpretation of the birth of architecture in Frank Lloyd Wright, The living City, Horizon Press, New York 1958.

[2] *Genesis* 4.12 and 4.15.

[3] *Genesis* 4.20-21.

[4] Bruce Chatwin, *The Songlines*, op. cit, p. 259.

[5] Richard Sennet, *The Conscience of the Eye: The Design and Social Life of Cities*, Knopf, New York 1992, p. 17.

[6] On the role of Sahel as a margin between nomadism and sedentaryism and the perception of emptiness in nomadic space, see Eugenio Turri: For the nomad - writes Turri - the desert smells of void and in this regard quotes a phrase from Lawrence: «This,» said the Arabs, «is the best perfume, it smells of nothing.» His life knew the air, the winds, the sun and the light, the open spaces, and an immense void. There was no fruitfulness in nature; no human effort appeared: only the sky on the top, the whole earth on the bottom. Nothing else.» Eugenio Turri, *Gli uomini delle tende...*, op cit., p.40.

[7] Gilles Deleuze and Félix Guattari, *Mille plateaux: capitalisme et schizophrénie*, Les Éditions de Minuit, Paris, 1980, p. 50. (English version: *A Thousand Plateaus: Capitalism and Schizophrenia*, Atholone Press, London, 1987).

Walkscapes — walking as an aesthetic practice

[8] On the walkabout of Aboriginal Australians in addition to Bruce Chatwin, *The Songlines...*, op. cit., see also: Franco La Cecla, *Perdersi, l'uomo senza ambiente*, Laterza, Bari 1988; Franco La Cecla, *Mente locale. Per un'antropologia dell'abitare*, elèuthera, Milano 1993; Barbara Glowczewski, *YAPA. Peintres aborigènes*, Baudoin Lebon, Paris 1991; Marlo Morgan, *Mutant Message Down Under*, MM Co. 1991; Kenneth White, *L'art de la terre*, in : "Ligeia" n°11-12, Paris 1992, p. 76; Theodor G.H. Strehlow, *Central Australian Religion. Personal Monototemism in a Polytotemic Community*, Flinders Press, South Australia 1993.

[9] On the nuragic and prenuragic history of Sardinia see: Giovanni Lilliu, *La civiltà dei sardi, dal paleolitico all'età dei nuraghi*, Nuova ERI, Torino 1963; Sergio Frau, *Le colonne d'Ercole. Un inchiesta*, neon, Roma 2002; Leonardo Melis, *Shardana. I popoli del mare*, PTM, Mogoro 2002; Enrico Atzeni, *La scoperta delle Statue-Menhir. Trent'anni di ricerche archeologiche nel territorio di Laconi*, Cuec, Cagliari 2004.

[10] See Michel Cazenave, *Enciclopédie de Simboles*, La Pochothèque L.G.F., Paris 1996; Jean Chevalier et Alain Gheerbrant, *Dictionnaire des Symboles*, Lafont/Jupiter, Paris 1969.

[11] On the spread of megalithicism see Paolo Malagrinò, *Dolmen e menhir di Puglia*, Schena, Fasano, 1982. On the location of menhirs along the intercontinental routes see Arthur Breizh, *Le ossa del drago. Sentieri magici dai menhir ai celti*, Keltia, Aosta 1996. On religious pilgrimages see Edith Turner e Victor Turner, *Image and Pilgrimage in Christian Culture*, Columbia University Press, New York 1978. For the youthful wandering of Buddha, Jesus and Muhammad see Odon Vallet, *Trois marcheurs: Bouddha, Jésus, Mahomet*, in: *Qu'est-ce qu'une route?*, "Les Cahiers de médiologie" n° 2, Paris 1997.

[12] There are many similarities between the Spatiality of the Karnak hypostyle in Egypt and the alignments of Carnac in Brittany, and their relationships with the Ka. I wrote more about it on Francesco Careri, *Pasear, detenerse*, Gustavo Gili, Barcelona 2016.

[13] On concepts of ka and benben and their relationship with the pyramids and the first Egyptian temples see Sigfried Giedion, *The Eternal Present. A Contribution on Constancy and Change*, Pantheon Books, New York, 1964; Serge Sauneron e Jean Yoyotte, *La Naissance du Monde*, in "Sources Orientales", vol. I, Paris 1959, pp. 82-83.

"The city is the realization of the ancient human dream of the labyrinth. Without knowing it, the *flâneur* is devoted to this reality. [...] Landscape, this is what the city becomes for the *flâneur*. Or more precisely: for him the city splits into its dialectical poles. It opens to him like a landscape and encloses him like a room."

WALTER BENJAMIN, *Das Passagen-Werk* [1929], Suhrkamp Verlag, Frankfurt am Main, 1983 (English version: *The Arcades Project*, Belknap Press, Cambridge, MA, 1999).

"Not to find one's way in a city may well be uninteresting and banal. It requires ignorance—nothing more. But to lose oneself in a city—as one loses oneself in a forest—that calls for quite a different schooling. Then, signboards and street names, passers-by, roofs, kiosks, or bars must speak to the wanderer like a cracking twig under his feet in the forest, like the startling call of a bittern in the distance."

WALTER BENJAMIN, *Berliner Kinderheit um Neunzehnhundert* [1930-1933], Suhrkamp Verlag, Frankfurt am Main, 1950. (English version: "A Berlin Chronicle", in *One-Way Street and Other Writings*, NLB, London, 1979).

Anti Walk

The Dada Visit

On 14 April 1921 in Paris, at three in the afternoon, in pouring rain, the Dada movement had an appointment to meet in front of the church of Saint-Julien-le-Pauvre. This action was to be the first in a series of urban excursions to the *banal places* of the city. It is a conscious aesthetic operation backed up by press releases, proclamations, flyers and photographic documentation. The visit opens the Grande Saison Dada, a season of public operations designed to give new energy to the group, which was in a moment of the doldrums and internal debate.[1] André Breton recalled the project as a substantial failure: "Passing from the halls of spectacle to the open air will not suffice to put an end to the Dada recyclings."[2] In spite of Breton's words, this first visit remains the most important Dada intervention in the city. The passage from the halls of spectacle to "the open air" was, in fact, the first step in a long series of excursions, deambulations and 'driftings' that crossed the entire century as a form of anti-art.

The first Dada urban readymade marks the passage from the representation of motion to the construction of an aesthetic action to be effected in the reality of everyday life. In the first years of the century the theme of motion had become one of the main areas of research of the avant-gardes. Movement and speed had emerged as a new urban presence capable of imprinting itself on the canvases of the painters and the pages of the poets. At first, attempts were made to capture movement with traditional means of representation. Later, after the Dada experience, there was a passage from the representation of motion to the practice of movement in real space. With the Dada visits and the subsequent deambulations of the Surrealists the action of passing through space was utilized as an aesthetic form capable of taking the place of representation, and therefore of the art system in general.

Dada effected the passage from the *representation* of the city of the future to the *habitation* of the city of the banal. The Futurist city was crossed by flows of energy and eddies of the human masses, a city that had lost any possibility of static vision, set in motion by the speeding vehicles, the lights and noises, the multiplication of perspective vantage points and the continuous metamorphosis of space.[3] But the research of the Futurists, though it was based on a sophisticated interpretation of the new urban spaces and the events that took place there, stopped at the phase of representation, without going beyond to penetrate the field of action. The act of exploration and acoustic, visual, and tactile perception of urban spaces in transformation was not considered an aesthetic action in its own right. The Futurists did not intervene in the urban environment; their soirées took place in literary circles, art galleries and theaters, and almost never (with the exception of brawls and political assemblies) in the reality of the city.

Tristan Tzara, in the manifesto of 1916, had declared that Dada is "decidedly against the future," indicating that every sort of possible universe is already available in the present. The urban actions performed in the early 1920s by the Parisian group that had formed around Breton were already very distant from the proclamations of the Futurists. The Dada city is a city of the banal that has abandoned all the hyper-technological utopias of Futurism. The frequentation and visiting of insipid places represented, for the Dadaists, a concrete way of arriving at the total secularization of art, so as to achieve a union between art and life, the sublime and the quotidian. It is interesting to note that the setting for the first Dada action is precisely

EXcuRSIoNs & VISITES **DADA**

UN CULTE NOUVEAU:

DISTRIBUTION DE BAS DE SOIE A 5,85

LA PROPRETÉ EST LE LUXE DU PAUVRE SOYEZ SALE

LEÇONS DE COUPE

DADA

1ÈRE *Église* **VISITE:**

Saint Julien le Pauvre

PROCHAINES VISITES:
Musée du Louvre
Buttes Chaumont
Gare Saint-Lazare
Mont du Petit Cadenas
Canal de l'Ourcq
etc.

JEUDI 14 AVRIL A 3 h.

RENDEZ-VOUS DANS LE JARDIN DE L'ÉGLISE

Rue Saint Julien le Pauvre — (Métro Saint-Michel et Cité)

ON DOIT COUPER SON NEZ COMME SES CHEVEUX

COURSES PÉDESTRES DANS LE JARDIN

Les dadaïstes de passage à Paris voulant remédier à l'incompétence de guides et de cicerones suspects, ont décidé d'entreprendre une série de visites à des endroits choisis, en particulier à ceux qui n'ont vraiment pas de raison d'exister. — C'est à tort qu'on insiste sur le pittoresque (Lycée Janson de Sailly), l'intérêt historique (Mont Blanc) et la valeur sentimentale (la Morgue). — La partie n'est pas perdue mais il faut agir vite. — Prendre part à cette première visite c'est se rendre compte du progrès humain, des destructions possibles et de la nécessité de poursuivre notre action que vous tiendrez à encourager par tous les moyens.

LAVEZ VOS SEINS COMME VOS GANTS

* EN BAS LE BAS ■——■ EN HAUT LE HAUT —■

Sous la conduite de: Gabrielle BUFFET, Louis ARAGON, ARP, André BRETON, Paul ELUARD, Th. FRAENKEL, J. HUSSAR, Benjamin PÉRET, Francis PICABIA, Georges RIBEMONT-DESSAIGNES, Jacques RIGAUT, Carla BODONI, Philippe SOUPAULT, Tristan TZARA.

MERCI POUR LE FUSIL

et encore une fois **BONJOUR**

(Le piano a été mis très gentiment à notre disposition par la maison Gaveau.)

Flyer distributed to passers-by "The Dadaists passing through Paris, as a remedy for the incompetence of guides and dubious pedants, have decided to undertake a series of visits to selected places, in particular to those places that do not truly have any reason to exist. It is incorrect to insist upon the picturesque, historical interest and sentimental value. The game has not yet been lost, but we must act quickly. Participation in this first visit means answering for human progress, for possible destructions and responding to the need to pursue our action, which you will attempt to encourage by any means possible."

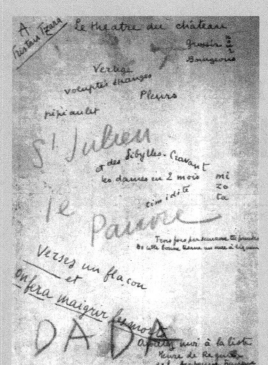

Working draft of the invitation for the first visit to Saint-Julien-le-Pauvre.

LE 14 AVRIL 1921

OUVERTURE

DE LA

GRANDE SAISON

DADA

VISITES · SALON DADA · CONGRÈS ·
COMMÉMORATIONS · OPÉRAS ·
PLÉBICISTES · RÉQUISITIONS ·
MISES EN ACCUSATION ET JUGEMENTS

Se faire inscrire au SANS PAREIL

Dada at Saint-Julien-le-Pauvre, Paris, 14 April 1921. From the left: Jean Crotti, Georges D'Esparbès, André Breton, Georges Rigaut, Paul Éluard, Georges Ribemont-Dessaignes, Benjamin Péret, Théodore Fraenkel, Louis Aragon, Tristan Tzara, Philippe Soupault. (Musée d'Art et d'Histoire de Saint Denis).

Press Release "Today at 3pm in the garden of the church of Saint-Julien-le-Pauvre [...] Dada inaugurates a series of Excursions in Paris, inviting friends and enemies alike to visit the *dépendances* of the church free of charge. It would appear, in fact, that something can still be discovered in the garden, in spite of its familiarity to tourists. This is not an anticlerical demonstration, as one might be tempted to believe, but rather a new interpretation of nature applied, this time, not to art but to life."

The Story as Told by André Breton
"The principle of the Dada events has not been abandoned. It is decided that the procedure will be different. To this end, a series of excursions or visits will be conducted in Paris, selected according to utterly gratuitous criteria. [...] In truth, the application of this program has only been roughly outlined. The meeting in the garden of Saint-Julien-le-Pauvre actually takes place, but it is hampered by pouring rain and, even more so, by the dreadful vapidness of the speeches made, pronounced in a deliberately provocative tone. It is not sufficient to leave the halls of spectacle for the open air in order to be finished with the Dada recyclings."

ANDRÉ PARINAUD (ed.), *André Breton-Entretiens*, Gallimard, Paris, 1952.

"The earth,
beneath my feet,
is nothing but an immense
open newspaper.
At times a photograph appears,
a curiosity like any other
and the flowers uniformly emit
the scent,
the good scent
of printer's ink."

ANDRÉ BRETON, Poisson soluble, Éditions du Sagittaire, Paris, 1924.

"The street I believed was capable of causing surprising turning-points in my life, the street, with its restlessness and its glances, was my true element: there, as in no other place, I received the winds of eventuality."

ANDRÉ BRETON, *Les pas perdus*, N.R.F., Paris, 1924 (English version: *Lost Steps*, MIT Press, Cambridge, MA, 1998).

"I move in a landscape where revolution and love speak overwhelming words."

RENÉ CHAR, "Poèmes (à Aragon)", in *Le Surréalisme au service de la révolution*, 3, December 1931 (English version: *Poems of René Char*, Princeton University Press, Princeton (N. J.), 1976).

modern Paris, the city already frequented, at the end of the previous century, by the *flâneur,* that ephemeral character who, in his rebellion against modernity, killed time by enjoying manifestations of the unusual and the absurd, when wandering about the city. Dada raised the tradition of *flânerie* to the level of an aesthetic operation. The Parisian walk described by Walter Benjamin in the 1920s is utilized as an art form that inscribes itself directly in real space and time, rather than on a medium. Paris, therefore, was the first city to offer itself as an ideal territory for those artistic experiences that sought to give life to the revolutionary project of going beyond art pursued by the Surrealists and the Situationists.[4]

The Urban *Readymade*

In 1917 Duchamp had proposed the Woolworth Building in New York as his own ready-made work, but this was still an architectonic object and not a public space. The urban readymade realized at Saint-Julien-le-Pauvre, on the other hand, is the first symbolic operation that attributes aesthetic value to a space rather than an object. Dada progressed from introducing a banal object into the space of art to introducing art—the persons and bodies of the Dada artists—into a banal place in the city. That "new interpretation of nature applied this time not to art, but to life," announced in the press release explaining the Saint-Julien-le-Pauvre operation, is a revolutionary appeal to life versus art and the quotidian versus the aesthetic, challenging the traditional modes of urban intervention, a field of action usually reserved for architects and town planners. Before the Dada action, artistic activity could be inserted in public space only through operations of decoration, such as the installation of sculptural objects in squares and parks. The Dada intervention offers artists a new possibility for working on the city. Before the Dada visit any artist who wanted to present a place to his audience had to shift the real place into a place designated by means of representation, with the inevitable consequence of a subjective interpretation.

Dada did not intervene in the place by inserting an object or by removing others. It brought the artist, or the group of artists, directly

74   *Walkscapes – walking as an aesthetic practice*

to the site in question, without effecting any material operation, without leaving physical traces other than the documentation of the operation—flyers, photographs, articles, stories—and without any kind of subsequent elaboration.

Among the photos documenting the event there is one showing the group in the garden of the church, perhaps the most important image of the entire operation. We see the Dada group posing on an untended patch of ground. The image shows none of the actions that had accompanied the event, such as the reading of texts selected at random from a Larousse dictionary, the giving of gifts to passers-by, or the attempts to get people to leave their homes and come into the street. The subject of the photo is the presence of that particular group in the city, aware of the action they are performing and conscious of what they are doing, namely *nothing*. The work lies in having thought of the action to perform, rather than in the action itself. Perhaps this is why the other actions in the program never took place. The project was not taken to its conclusion because it was already finished. Having performed the action in that particular place was the equivalent of having performed it on the entire city. We don't know which of the Dada artists had suggested that site—"an abandoned church, known to few people, surrounded at the time by a sort of *terrain vague* enclosed by fences"—nor the reasons behind the choice.

But its position, in the heart of the Latin Quarter, seems to indicate that this particular garden around a church was selected precisely as if it were an abandoned garden near one's own home: a space to investigate, familiar but unknown, seldom visited but evident, a banal, useless space which like so many others *wouldn't really have any reason to exist*. The exploration of the city and the continuing discovery of situations to investigate is possible anywhere, even in the heart of Parisian tourism zones, even along the Seine on the *rive gauche* facing the cathedral of Notre Dame. With the exploration of the banal, Dada launched the application of Freud's research to the unconscious of the city. This idea was later to be developed by the Surrealists and the Situationists.[5]

The story of Deambulation, as told by André Breton "We all agree, then, that a grand adventure is at hand.

'Let everything go… Set forth on the roads': this was the motif of my exhortations in that period. [...] But which roads? On material roads? Not very probable. On spiritual roads? We didn't like the sound of it. The fact remains that we got the idea of combining these two types of roads.

This led to the deambulation in quartet, Aragon, Morise, Vitrac and I, in approximately this season, starting from Blois, a town we selected randomly from the map.

We agreed to proceed by chance, on foot, continuing to converse, not allowing ourselves deliberate detours unless they were necessary for eating and sleeping. The performing of this project turned out to be quite singular and even fraught with dangers. The journey, planned to last about ten days and later shortened, suddenly took on a tone of adepts.

The absence of any purpose soon detached us from reality, causing more and more ghosts, increasingly disquieting, to be raised by our steps. Irritation was always lurking in the wings, and Aragon and Vitrac even came to blows.

All things considered, by no means a disappointing exploration, in spite of the small radius covered, because it was an exploration at the confines between conscious life and dream life, and therefore to the greatest degree in tune with our concerns of that time."

ANDRÉ PARINAUD (ed.), *André Breton - Entretiens*, Gallimard, Paris, 1952.

PUBLICITÉ   PUBLICITÉ

GIL J WOLMAN présente

Le mouvement lettriste n'a pas fini son strip-tease
Visitez PARIS PSYCHOGÉOGRÁPHIQUE
Le hasard vous guide LA DÉRIVE vous perd
Les SITUATIONS confuses sont mal CONSTRUITES

UNE AVENTURE
D'AMOUR ET DE MORT
DANS LE CADRE
PRESTIGIEUX
DES ILES

L'architecture la plus fâcheuse est celle que propage

FIRMIN LE CORBUSIER

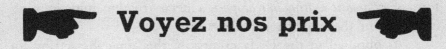 **Voyez nos prix**

SEE RED   INTERNATIONALE LETTRISTE
32, rue de la Montagne-Geneviève, PARIS Vᵉ

GIL J. WOLMAN, "Publicité", in *Les Lèvres nues*, 7, 1955.

Surrealist Deambulation

Three years after the Dada visit, in May 1924, the Paris Dada group organized another intervention in real space. This time, instead of an encounter in a selected place in the city, the plan was for an erratic journey in a vast natural territory. The voyage is the materialization of the *lâchez tout* of Breton, a veritable path of initiation that marks the definitive passage from Dada to Surrealism. In this period the Dada events were beginning to meet with less enthusiasm, relations with Tristan Tzara were deteriorating, and a need was felt to gather energy and prepare for a new breakthrough. It was in this delicate moment that Louis Aragon, André Breton, Max Morise and Roger Vitrac organized a deambulation in open country in the center of France. The group decided to set forth from Paris, going to Blois, a small town selected randomly on the map, by train and then continuing on foot as far as Romorantin. Breton recalled this "quartet deambulation," conversing and walking for many consecutive days, as an "exploration between waking life and dream life."[6] After returning from the trip he wrote the introduction to *Poisson soluble,* which was to become the first Surrealist Manifesto, in which we find the first definition of the term Surrealism: "pure psychic automatism with which one aims at expressing, whether verbally or in writing, or in any other way, the real functioning of thought."[7] The trip, undertaken without aim or destination, had been transformed into a form of *automatic writing in real space,* a literary/rural roaming imprinted directly on the map of a mental territory.

As opposed to the Dada excursion, this time the setting for the action is not the city, but an 'empty' territory. The *deambulation*—a term that already contains the essence of disorientation and self-abandon to the unconscious—took place amidst woods, countryside, paths, and small rural settlements. It would appear that the aim of going beyond the real into the dream world was accompanied by a desire for a return to vast, uninhabited spaces, at the limits of real space. The Surrealist path was positioned out of time, crossing the childhood of the world, taking on the archetypal forms of wandering in the empathic territories of the primitive universe. Space appears as an active, pulsating subject, an autonomous producer of affections and relations. It is a living organism with its own character, a counterpart with shifting moods, with which it is possible to establish a relationship of mutual exchange. The path unwinds amidst snares and dangers, provoking a strong state of *apprehension* in the person walking, in both senses of 'feeling fear' and 'grasping' or 'learning.' This empathic territory penetrates down to the deepest strata of the mind, evoking images of other worlds in which reality and nightmare live side by side, transporting the being into a state of unconsciousness where the ego is no longer definite. Deambulation is the achievement of a state of hypnosis by walking, a disorienting loss of control. It is a medium through which to enter into contact with the unconscious part of the territory.

City as Amniotic Fluid

Just as the other excursions announced by Dada were never completed, so the rural wanderings of the Surrealists happened only once. But the continuing deambulation in groups through the outskirts of Paris—an interminable stroll, as Jacques Baron called it—did become one of the most assiduously practiced activities of the Surrealists for investigating that unconscious part of the city that eluded bourgeois transformation.

In 1924 Louis Aragon published *Le Paysan de Paris,* whose title seems to be the inversion of the rural excursion. While previously four Parisians got lost in the countryside, now the city is described from the viewpoint of a *paysan,* a peasant who must grapple with the *vertigo of the modern* provoked by the nascent metropolis. The book is a sort of guide to the quotidian marvels concealed inside the modern city. It is the description of those unknown places and fragments of life that unfold far from tourist itineraries, in a sort of submerged, undecipherable universe. During a nocturnal deambulation, the Park of Buttes-Chaumont is described as the place "where the unconscious of the city lurks," a terrain of experiences where it is possible to meet up with extraordinary surprises and revelations.[8]

In *Le Paysan de Paris,* Mirella Bandini finds a "recurring simile of the sea, of its mobile, labyrinthine space, its vastness; like the sea,

Paris has the sense of the maternal womb and of nourishing liquid, of incessant agitation, of a totality."[9] It is in this *amniotic fluid,* where everything grows and is spontaneously transformed, out of sight, that the endless walks, the encounters, the *trouvailles* (discoveries of *objets trouvés*), the unexpected events, and collective games happen. These early deambulations led to the idea of giving form to the perception of the space of the city in *cartes influentielles* that take their place alongside the vision of the liquid city in Situationist cartography. The idea was to make maps based on the variations of perception obtained when walking through the urban environment, to include the *impulses* caused by the city in the *affective sentiments* of the pedestrian. Breton believed in the possibility of drawing maps in which the places we like are in white, the places we try to avoid in black, while the rest, in gray, would represent the zones in which sensations of attraction and repulsion alternate. These sensations regarding certain settings could be perceived, for example, walking down a familiar street where "if we pay the slightest bit of attention we can recognize zones of well-being and malaise that alternate, for which we could determine the respective lengths."[10]

From Banal City to Unconscious City

The Futurist city of flux and speed had been transformed by Dada into a place in which to notice the banal and the ridiculous, in which to unmask the farce of the bourgeois city, a public place in which to thumb noses at institutional culture. The Surrealists abandoned the nihilism of Dada and moved toward a positive project. Using the groundwork laid by nascent psychoanalytical theory, they plunged beyond Dadaist negation in the conviction that "something is hidden behind there." Beyond the territories of the banal exist the territories of the unconscious, beyond negation the discovery of a new world that must be investigated before being rejected or greeted with mere derision. The Surrealists believed that urban space could be crossed like our mind, that a non-visible reality can reveal itself in the city. The Surrealist research is a sort of psychological investigation of one's relationship with urban reality, an operation already applied with

Walkscapes – walking as an aesthetic practice

success through automatic writing and hypnotic dreams, and which can also be directly applied in walking through the city.

The Surrealist city is an organism that produces and conceals territories to be explored, landscapes in which to get lost and to endlessly experience the sensation of *everyday wonder*.

Dada had glimpsed the fact that the city could be an aesthetic space in which to operate through quotidian/symbolic actions, and had urged artists to abandon the usual forms of representation, pointing the way toward direct intervention in public space. Surrealism, perhaps without yet fully understanding its importance as an aesthetic form, utilized walking—the most natural and everyday act of man—as a means by which to investigate and unveil the *unconscious zones of the city*, those parts that elude planned control and constitute the unexpressed, untranslatable component in traditional representations. The Situationists were to accuse the Surrealists of failing to take the potential of the Dada project to its extreme consequences. The 'artless,' art without artwork or artist, the rejection of representation and personal talent, the pursuit of an anonymous, collective and revolutionary art, would be combined, along with the practice of walking, in the wandering of the Lettrist/Situationists.

Dérive versus Deambulation "The *dérive* entails play-ful-constructive behavior and an awareness of psychogeo-graphical effects; which completely distinguishes it from the classical notions of the *journey* and the *stroll*. An insufficient awareness of the limitations of chance, and of its inevitably reactionary use, condemned to a dismal failure the celebrat-ed aimless *ambulation* attempted in 1923 by four Surreal-ists, beginning from a town chosen by lot: *wandering* in the open country is naturally depressing, and the interventions of chance are poorer there than anywhere else."

GUY DEBORD, "Théorie de la dérive", in *Les Lèvres nues*, 8/9, 1956, and reprinted in 1958 in *Internationale Situationniste*, 2 (English version: LIBERO ANDREOTTI & XAVIER COSTA (eds.), *Theory of the Dérive and other Situationist Writings on the City*, Museu d'Art Contemporani de Barcelona/Actar, Barcelona, 1996).

In girum imus nocte et consumimur igni

"The phrase that reverses itself, constructed letter by letter like a labyrinth, perfectly represents the form and the content of perdition."

"We have not sought the formula for turning the world upside-down in books, but by wandering around. [...] Together with four or five rather disreputable persons. [...] We have not gone on television to tell of the things we have understood. We have not aspired to receive grants for scientific research, nor the praise of the intellectuals. We have brought oil where there was fire."

GUY DEBORD, *Œuvres cinématographiques complètes,* Gallimard, Paris, 1994. The Latin phrase, attributed to the orator Sidonius Apollinaire, is a palindrome, or a phrase that reads identically forwards or backwards. The translation is "we spend the night wandering and the fire consumes us."

"Constructed situation A moment of life concretely and deliberately constructed by the collective organization of a unitary ambiance and a game of events.

Psychogeography The study of the specific effects of the geographical environment, consciously organized or not, on the emotions and behavior of individuals.

Dérive A mode of experimental behavior linked to the conditions of urban society: a technique of transient passage through varied ambiances. Also used to designate a specific period of continuous 'dériving'."

Unsigned, "Definitions", in *Internationale Situationniste*, 1, 1958 (English version: LIBERO ANDREOTTI & XAVIER COSTA (eds.), *op. cit.*).

"Architecture The simplest means of *articulating* time and space, of *modulating* reality, of engendering dreams. It is a matter not only of plastic articulation and modulation expressing an ephemeral beauty, but of a modulation producing influences in accordance with the eternal spectrum of human desires and the progress in realizing them.
The architecture of tomorrow will be a means of modifying present conceptions of time and space. It will be a *means of knowledge* and a *means of action*.
The architectural complex will be modifiable. Its aspect will change totally or partially in accordance with the will of its inhabitants..."

IVAN CHTCHEGLOV (alias GILLES IVAIN), "Formulary for a New Urbanism" (1953), reprinted in *Internationale Situationniste*, 1, 1958 (English version: LIBERO ANDREOTTI & XAVIER COSTA (eds.), *op. cit.*).

DESCRIPTION RAISONNÉE DE PARIS
(Itinéraire pour une nouvelle agence de voyages)

Le centre de Paris est la région de la Contrescarpe, de forme ovale, dont on peut suivre le pourtour en trois heures de marche environ. Sa partie nord est constituée par la Montagne-Geneviève; le terrain descend en pente douce vers le sud. Les habitants sont très pauvres, et généralement d'origine nord-africaine. C'est là que se rencontrent les émissaires de diverses puissances mal connues.

A une heure de marche vers le sud, on parvient à la Butte-aux-Cailles, d'un climat doux et tempéré. Les habitants sont très pauvres, mais la disposition des rues tend à la somptuosité d'un labyrinthe.

A quarante-cinq minutes de marche en direction de l'ouest, on trouve fréquemment, de 19 heures 30 à 8 heures, un square dépeuplé, d'une topographie surprenante, communément nommé « square des Missions Etrangères ».

A trente minutes de marche vers le nord-est, plusieurs passages parallèles, qui ne mènent nulle part, délimitent une petite agglomération chinoise. Les habitants sont très pauvres. Ils préparent des mets compliqués, peu nutritifs et fortement épicés.

Au nord-ouest, à une journée de marche, s'étend le désert de Retz, d'un abord extrêmement difficile, peuplé de rares indigènes sauvages et tard venus. Dans cette contrée peu sûre, la légèreté n'est pas de mise. Au cœur du désert de Retz on découvre les célèbres « fabriques », le chef-d'œuvre architectural du dix-huitième siècle, arbitrairement édifiées parmi la luxuriante végétation ambiante, à seules fins de jeux spontanément psychogéographiques.

A cinquante minutes de marche au nord de la Contrescarpe, après avoir traversé une île pratiquement déserte, appelée depuis très longtemps « île Louis », on rencontre un bar isolé, lieu de réunion constant des Polonais. Ils sont très pauvres. De sorte qu'on y trouve une vodka excellente pour un prix modique.

En poursuivant la route vers le nord, à deux heures de marche, on arrive au lieudit « Aubervilliers », plaine coupée de canaux inutilisables. Le climat y est froid, les chutes de neige fréquentes. Le jeu de la grenouille s'y pratique. Les habitants, très pauvres, parlent naturellement l'espagnol. Ils attendent la révolution. Ils jouent de la guitare et ils chantent.

Tels sont les intérêts de la dérive bien menée.

Jacques FILLON

JACQUES FILLON, "Description raisonnée de Paris (Itinéraire pour une nouvelle agence de voyages)", in *Les Lèvres nues*, 7, 1955.

Lettrist Drifting (*Dérive*)

In the early 1950s the Lettrist International, which became the Situationist International in 1957, saw getting lost in the city as a concrete expressive possibility of anti-art, adopting it as an aesthetic-political means by which to undermine the postwar capitalist system.

After the Dada 'visit' and the Surrealist 'deambulation' a new term was coined: the *dérive*, literally 'drift,' a recreational collective act that not only aims at defining the unconscious zones of the city, but which—with the help of the concept of 'psychogeography'—attempts to investigate the psychic effects of the urban context on the individual. The *dérive* is the construction and implementation of new forms of behavior in real life, the realization of an alternative way of inhabiting the city, a lifestyle situated outside and against the rules of bourgeois society, with the aim of going beyond the deambulation of the Surrealists. Apart from having conducted their deambulation in the country rather than the city, the Surrealists are defined as 'imbeciles' for not having understood—though it was right under their noses—the potential of deambulation as a collective art form, as an aesthetic operation that, if performed in a group, had the power to annul the individual components of the artwork, a fundamental concept for Dada and Surrealism. The *miserable failure* of the Surrealist deambulation was due, according to the Situationists, to the exaggerated importance assigned to the *unconscious* and to *chance,* categories that were still included in the Lettrists' practice, but in a diluted form, closer to reality, within a constructed method of investigation whose field of action must be life, and therefore the real city. Lettrist drifting develops the subjective interpretation of the city already begun by the Surrealists, but with the aim of transforming it into an objective method of exploration of the city: the urban space is an *objective passional terrain* rather than merely *subjective-unconscious.*

In Surrealism, attempts to realize a new use of life effectively coexisted with a reactionary flight from the real. And in this sense the importance attributed to dreams is interpreted by the Lettrists as the result of a bourgeois incapacity to realize a new lifestyle in the real world. The construction of the situation and the practice of the *dérive* are based, instead, on concrete control of the means and forms of behavior that can be directly experienced in the city. The Lettrists rejected the idea of a separation between alienating, boring real life and a marvelous imaginary life: reality itself had to become marvelous. It was no longer the time to celebrate the unconscious of the city, it was time to experiment with superior ways of living through the construction of situations in everyday reality: it was time to act, not to dream.

The practice of walking in a group, lending attention to unexpected stimuli, passing entire nights bar-hopping, discussing, dreaming of a revolution that seemed imminent, became a form of rejection of the system for the Lettrists: a means of escaping from bourgeois life and rejecting the rules of the art system. The *dérive* was, in fact, an action that would have a hard time fitting into the art system, as it consisted in constructing the modes of a situation whose consumption left no traces. It was a fleeting action, an immediate instant to be experienced in the present moment without considering its representation and conservation in time. An aesthetic activity that fit perfectly into the Dada logic of anti-art.

The drifting of the Lettrists, which began as juvenile perdition in the Parisian nights, over time took on the character of an antagonistic theory. In 1952 a small group of young writers, including Guy Debord, Gil Wolman, Michèle Bernstein, Mohamed Dahou, Jacques Fillon and Gilles Ivain, broke away from the Lettrism of Isidore Isou to found the Lettrist International "to work on the conscious, collective construction of a new civilization." The focus of their interest was no longer poetry, but a passionate way of living that took the form of adventure in the urban environment:

> Poetry has consumed its ultimate formalisms. Beyond aesthetics, poetry lies entirely in the power men will have in their adventures. Poetry is read on faces. Therefore it is urgent to create new faces. Poetry is in the form of the cities. We construct subversion. The new beauty will be that of the situation, temporary and experienced. [...] Poetry simply means the development of absolutely new forms of behavior and the means with which to be impassioned.[11]

Guy Debord, *Métagraphie, Mort de J. H. au fragiles tissues (en souvenir de Kaki)*, 1954

IVAN CHTCHEGLOV (alias GILLES IVAIN), Métagraphie, 1952.

GIL J. WOLMAN, Métagraphie, 1954.

Next spread: ASGER JORN, a page from *Fin de Copenhague*, 1957.

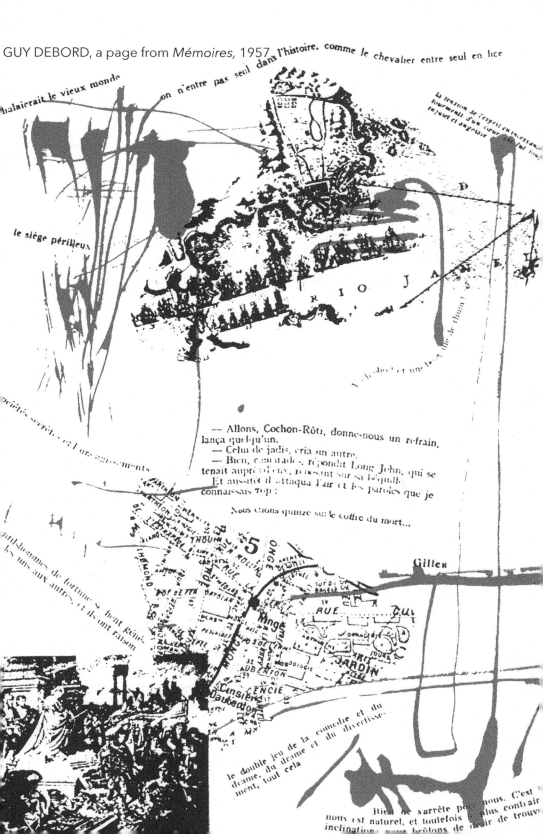

GUY DEBORD, a page from *Mémoires*, 1957

The Theory of the *Dérive*

In the years preceding the formation of the Situationist International, the Lettrists begin to develop a theory based on the practice of urban drifting. The time spent in marginal zones and the description of the unconscious city in Surrealist writings became a widespread literary genre in the mid-1950s, evolving into the Lettrist texts under the guise of travel guides and manuals for using the city. In 1955 Jacques Fillon wrote his *Description raisonnée de Paris (Itinéraire pour une nouvelle agence de voyages)*, a short guide with exotic, multi-ethnic itineraries to be completed on foot, from the departure point of the Lettrist headquarters on the Place Contrescarpe. But the first essay in which the term *dérive* appears is the *Formulaire pour un urbanisme nouveau,* written in 1953 by the 19-year-old Ivan Chtcheglov (alias Gilles Ivain) who, convinced of the fact that "a rational extension of [...] psychoanalysis into architectural expression becomes more and more urgent," describes a mutant city continuously varied by its inhabitants in which "the main activity of the inhabitants will be CONTINUOUS DRIFTING. The changing of landscapes from one hour to the next will result in total disorientation," through quarters whose names correspond to continuously changing moods.[12]

Guy Debord is the figure who collated these stimuli and completed the research. In 1955 he wrote his *Introduction a une critique de la géographie urbaine,* in which he set out to define experimental methods for "the observation of certain processes of the random and the predictable in the streets,"[13] while in 1956 with the *Théorie de la dérive* a definitive step was taken beyond the Surrealist deambulation. As opposed to the Surrealists' expedition, in the *dérive* "chance is a less important factor [...] than one might think: from a *dérive* point of view cities have psychogeographical contours, with constant currents, fixed points and vortices that strongly discourage entry into or exit from certain zones." The *dérive* is a constructed operation that accepts chance, but is not based on it. In fact it has a few rules: preparatory decision, based on psychogeographic maps of the directions of penetration of the environmental unit to be analyzed; the extension of the space of investigation can vary from the block to the quarter, to a maximum of "the complex of a large city and its peripheral zones;" the *dérive* can be effected in groups composed of two or three people who have reached the same level of awareness, since "cross-checking these different groups' impressions makes it possible to arrive at more objective conclusions;" the average duration is defined as one day, but can extend to weeks or months, taking the influence of climate variations, the possibility of pauses, the idea of taking a taxi to increase personal disorientation into account. Debord then continues, listing other urban operations like the "static *dérive* of an entire day in the Gare Saint-Lazare," or the

> possible appointment [...] and certain amusements of dubious taste that have always been enjoyed among our entourage—slipping by night into houses undergoing demolition, hitchhiking non-stop and without destination through Paris during a transportation strike in the name of adding to the confusion, wandering in subterranean catacombs forbidden to the public.[14]

L'Archipel Influentiel

On 11 June 1954 at the Galerie du Passage the Lettrist exhibition "66 métagraphies influentielles" was opened. The theory of the *dérive* aimed "to describe a previously lacking influential cartography," whose precedents are found in the writings of Breton. The *Métagraphies influentielles* of Gil J. Wolman are collages of images and phrases cut out of newspapers, while the work by Gilles Ivain is a map of Paris on which fragments of islands, archipelagos, and peninsulas cut out of a globe are placed: the *elsewhere* is everywhere, even in Paris, the exotic always within arm's reach; all you need to do is get lost and explore your own city. Three years later, in 1957, as preparatory documents for the founding of the Situationist International, Jorn and Debord continued the direction of the "metagraphs" in the books *Fin de Copenhague* and *Mémoires*. The informal marks of Jorn simulate the Danish coasts inhabited by symbols of consumption, while in the urban *mémoires* and amnesias of Debord the spurts of paint seem like *dérive* trails across fragments of city.

RALPH RUMNEY, *The Leaning Tower of Venice/Guide psychogéographique de Venise*, picture story, 1958.

tudy were taken at
ck line on the map,
ajectory through th
hogeographic intere

This view of Venice(pop:density 2.1/sq
metre)shows road-rail bridge from Ital
y,rail terminal,cemetery isle(arrow) a
nd distant Lido,playground of the idle
rich!

author
ients f
eymoon
ets joi

'A' is aware of photographer
and is showing off.Neverthel
ess environment is clearly a
ffecting his play-pattern.

gh Play and Game are not ay
ous, photo left shows they
not always contradictory.

Once again, in the images it is Debord who sums things up: the first true Situationist psychogeographical map is his *Guide psychogéographique de Paris.* It is conceived as a folding map to be distributed to tourists, but a map that invites its user to get lost. As in the Dada visits and the guide of Jacques Fillon, Debord too uses the imagery of tourism to describe the city. Opening this strange guide we find Paris exploded in pieces, a city whose unity has been utterly lost and in which we can recognize only fragments of the historical center floating in empty space. The hypothetical tourist is instructed to follow the arrows that connect homogeneous *environmental units* based on psychogeographical surveys. The city has been filtered by subjective experience, "measuring" on oneself and in comparison with others the affections and passions that take form by visiting places and listening to one's own inner impulses.

That same year Debord published another map, *The Naked City: Illustration de l'hypothèse des plaques tournantes en psychogéographique.* The city is nude, stripped by the *dérive,* and its garments float out of context. The disoriented quarters are continents set adrift in a liquid space, *passional* terrains that wander, attracting or repulsing one another due to the continuous production of disorienting affective tensions. The definition of the parts, the distances between the plates and the thicknesses of the vectors are the result of experienced states of mind.

In the two maps the routes inside the quarters are not indicated, the plates are islands that can be crossed completely, while the arrows are fragments of all the possible *dérives,* trajectories in the void, mental wanderings between memories and absences. Amidst the floating quarters there is the empty territory of urban amnesia. The unity of the city can be achieved only through the connection of fragmentary memories. The city is a psychic landscape constructed by means of *holes,* entire parts are forgotten or intentionally suppressed to construct an infinity of possible cities in the void. It seems that the *dérive* has begun to form affective vortices in the city, that the continuous generation of passions has allowed the continents to take on their own magnetic autonomy and to undertake their own *dérive* through a liquid space. The Paris of Aragon had already been an immense sea in which spontaneous life forms appeared as in an amniotic fluid, and islands and continents had already appeared in the metagraph of Gilles Ivain. But in the maps of Debord the figure of reference, at this point, is clearly the archipelago: a series of city-islands immersed in an empty sea furrowed by wandering. Many of the terms utilized make reference to this: the floating plates, the islands, the currents, the vortices and, above all, the term *dérive* in its meaning of 'drifting,' without direction, at the mercy of the waters, and the nautical meaning as a part of a boat, the leeboard, an enlargement and extension of the keel that makes it possible to go against the current and to steer. The rational and the irrational, conscious and unconscious meet in the term *dérive*. Constructed wandering produces new territories to be explored, new spaces to be inhabited, new routes to be run. As the Lettrists had announced, roaming will lead "to the conscious, collective construction of a new civilization."

Playful City versus Bourgeois City

The Situationists replaced the unconscious dream city of the Surrealists with a *playful,* spontaneous city. While conserving the tendency to look for the repressed memories of the city, the Situationists replaced the randomness of Surrealist roaming with the construction of *rules of the game.* To play means deliberately breaking the rules and *inventing* your own, to free creative activity from socio-cultural restrictions, to design aesthetic and revolutionary actions that undermine or elude social control. The theory of the Situationists was based on an aversion for work and the premise of an imminent transformation of the *use of time* in society: with the changes in production systems and the progress of automation, work time would be reduced in favor of *free time.* Therefore it was important to protect the use of this non-productive time from the powers that be. Otherwise it would be sucked into the system of capitalist consumption through the creation of induced needs. This is the very description of the process of spectacularization of space in progress today, in which workers must also produce more in their free time, consuming their income inside the system. If recreational time was increasingly being transformed into a time of passive consumption, free time would have to become a time

ÉDITÉ PAR LE BAUHAUS IMAGINISTE

PRINTED IN DENMARK BY
PERMILD & ROSENGREEN

GUIDE PSYCHOGEOGRAPHIQUE DE PARIS

DISCOURS SUR LES PASSIONS DE L'AMOUR

pentes psychogeographiques de la dérive et localisation
d'unites d'ambiance

par G.-E. DEBORD

GUY DEBORD, *Guide psychogéographique de Paris*, 1957.

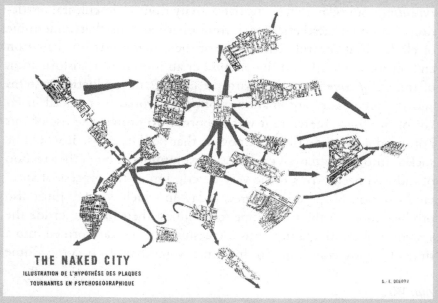

THE NAKED CITY

ILLUSTRATION DE L'HYPOTHÉSE DES PLAQUES
TOURNANTES EN PSYCHOGEOGRAPHIQUE

G.-E. DEBORD

GUY DEBORD, *The Naked City*, 1957.

"In Paris we wandered from café to café, we went where our steps and our inclinations led us. We had to make due with very little money. I still wonder how we managed. We did *dérives* in Paris in an extremely limited zone. We discovered routes to go from one place to another that were more like detours. [...] For me, Paris at length remained a perimeter enclosed by Montparnasse, Saint-Germain-des-Prés and the Rue de la Huchette. Every time we went out it was an adventure. [...] You discover certain places in the city and you start to appreciate them because they treat you nicely in a bar or because you suddenly feel better. This has a relationship with the sensation you feel for one place rather than another. As Debord has written, if you set off on a *dérive* in the right frame of mind, you will certainly wind up in the right place."

GERARD BERRÉBY, *Ralph Rumney, Le Consul,* Éditions Allia, Paris, 1999.

devoted to *play*, not utilitarian but ludic.[15] Therefore it was urgent to prepare a revolution based on *desire*: to seek the latent desires of people in the everyday world, stimulating them, re-awakening them, helping them to take the place of the wants imposed by the dominant culture. By making use of time and space it would be possible to escape the rules of the system and to achieve and self-construct new spaces of liberty. The Situationist slogan would come true: "living is being at home wherever you go." The *construction of situations* was therefore the most direct way to realize new forms of behavior in the city, and to experience the moments of what life could be in a freer society within urban reality.

The Situationists saw the psychogeographical *dérive* as the means with which to strip the city naked, but also with which to construct a playful way of reclaiming its territory: the city is a toy to be utilized at one's pleasure, a space for collective living, for the experience of alternative behaviors, a place in which to *waste useful time* so as to transform it into playful-constructive time. It was necessary to challenge that affluence-peddled-as-happiness by bourgeois propaganda, which took the form in urban terms of the construction of houses with "all mod[ern] con[venience]s" and the organization of mobility. It was necessary to "go from the concept of circulation as a supplement of work and distribution in the various functional zones of the city to one of circulation as pleasure and adventure,"[16] to experience the city as a playful territory to be utilized for the circulation of men toward an authentic life. What was needed was the construction of adventures.

World as a Nomadic Labyrinth

Through Constant's New Babylon the theory of the *dérive* simultaneously acquired a historical basis and a three-dimensional architectural form. In 1956, in Alba, where Asger Jorn and Pinot Gallizio had set up the Experimental Laboratory of the Imaginist Bauhaus, nomadism inserted itself in the history of architecture as a critique of the foundations of occidental society, ushering in a new territory of development for the architectural avant-gardes of the decades to follow.[17]

Walkscapes – walking as an aesthetic practice

Visiting a camp of nomads on land owned by Pinot Gallizio, Constant found an entire conceptual apparatus with which he felt it possible to refute the sedentary bases of functionalist architecture. He began working on a project for the gypsies of Alba and soon was able to imagine a city designed for a new nomadic society, "a planetary-scale nomadic camp."[18] The series of models he built until the mid-1970s represent the vision of a world which, after the revolution, would be inhabited by the descendants of Abel, by *Homo Ludens* who, free of the slavery of labor, could explore and at the same time transform the landscape around him. New Babylon is a playful city, a collective work built by the architectural creativity of a new errant society, a population that infinitely builds and rebuilds its own labyrinth in a new artificial landscape. The project of New Babylon was developed together with the Situationist theory of *unitary urbanism,* a new creative activity of transformation of urban space that takes the Dada myth of "going beyond art" and shifts it into an initial attempt to "go beyond architecture." In unitary urbanism all the arts combine in the construction of the space of man. The inhabitants would rediscover the primordial aptitude for self-determination of one's environment, rediscovering the instinct for the construction of one's own home and one's own life. The architect, like the artist, would have to change jobs: no longer the builder of isolated forms, but the builder of complete environments, of the scenarios of a waking dream. Architecture would thus become part of a wider-ranging activity, and like the other arts it would disappear in favor of a unified activity that sees the urban environment as the relational ground for a game of participation.[19]

Constant said: "For over half a century the world has been filled by the spirit of Dada. Seen in this perspective perhaps New Babylon could be called a *response* to anti-art."[20] Constant came to terms with nomadism and Dada in the attempt to go beyond both. He had a dual objective: to go beyond anti-art and to construct a nomadic city. Giulio Carlo Argan, to explain the essence of Dada, had written: "An artistic movement that negates art is a contradiction: Dada is this contradiction."[21] On the subject of New Babylon we might say the same thing: "To design a city for a nomadic people that negates the city is a contradiction: New Babylon is this contradiction." A double negative leads to a positive solution: a mega-structural, labyrinthine architecture, based on the sinuous line of the nomad's journey. One step back into the Neolithic, one step forward into the future. For the first time in history, in New Babylon walking again materializes an architecture conceived as the *space of going*. The unitary urbanism of Constant gives rise to a new Situationist city. While in the maps of Debord the compact city was exploded into pieces, in those of Constant the pieces are put back together to form a new city. There is no longer a separation between the clumps of urban sod and the empty sea crisscrossed by the trails of the *dérive*. In New Babylon the *dérive*, local areas, and empty space have become an inseparable whole. The 'plates' of Debord have become 'sectors' connected in a continuous sequence of different cities and heterogeneous cultures. The inhabitants of the entire world can get lost in these labyrinths. The entire city is imagined as a single space for continuous drifting. It is no longer a sedentary city rooted to the ground, but a nomadic city suspended in the air, a horizontal Tower of Babel looming over immense territories to envelop the entire surface of the earth. Nomadism and city have become a single huge labyrinthine corridor that travels around the world. A hyper-technological and multi-ethnic city that is constantly transforming itself in space and time:

> New Babylon doesn't end anywhere (because the Earth is round); it knows no boundaries (as there are no national economies) or collective life (as humanity is always moving). Each place is accessible to one and all. The entire Earth becomes a home for its inhabitants. Life is an infinite voyage through a world that is changing so rapidly that it always seems like another.[22]

Walkscapes – walking as an aesthetic practice

"The urbanists of the twentieth century will have to construct adventures. The simplest Situationist act would consist in abolishing all the memories of the employment of time of our epoch. It is an epoch which, up until now, has lived far below its means."

Unsigned, "Unitary Urbanism at the end of the 1950s", in *Internationale Situationniste*, 3, 1959 (English version: LIBERO ANDREOTTI & XAVIER COSTA (eds.), *op. cit.*).

"The new forces orient themselves towards a complex of human activities which extend beyond utility: leisure, superior games. Contrary to what the functionalists think, culture is situated at the point where usefulness ends."

A. ALBERTS, ARMANDO, CONSTANT, HAR OUDEJANS, "First Proclamation of the Dutch Section of IS", in *Internationale Situationniste*, 3, 1959 (English version: LIBERO ANDREOTTI & XAVIER COSTA (eds.), *op. cit.*).

"For many a year the gypsies who stopped a while in the little Piedmontese town of Alba were in the habit of camping
beneath the roof that once a week, on Saturday, housed the
livestock market. There they lit their fires, hung their tents
from the pillars to protect or isolate themselves, improvised
shelters with the aid of boxes and planks left behind by the
traders. The need to clean up the market place every time
the Zingari passed through had led the Town Council to for-
bid them access. In compensation they were assigned a bit
of grassland on the banks of the Tamaro, the little river that
goes through the town: the most miserable of patches! It's
there that in December 1956 I went to see them in the com-
pany of the painter Pinot Gallizio, the owner of this uneven,
muddy, desolate terrain, who'd given it to them. They'd
closed off the space between some caravans with planks
and petrol cans, they'd made an enclosure, a 'gypsy town'.
That was the day I conceived the scheme for a permanent
encampment for the gypsies of Alba and that project is the
origin of the series of maquettes of New Babylon. Of a New
Babylon where under one roof, with the aid of moveable elements, a shared residence is built; a temporary, constantly
remodeled living area; a camp for nomads on a planetary
scale."

CONSTANT, *New Babylon*, Haags Gemeentemuseum, The Hague, 1974.

CONSTANT, Ontwerp voor Zigeunerkamp (Project for a Gypsy Camp), maquette, 1957.

CONSTANT, *Symbolische voorstelling van New Babylon* (Symbolic Representation of New Babylon), collage, 1969.

"We are the living symbols of a world without frontiers, of a world of freedom, free of weapons, where each one can travel without constraints from the plains of central Asia to the Atlantic coast, from the high plateaus of South Africa to the Finnish forests."

Vaida Voivod III, President of the World Community of Gypsies. Algmeen Handelsblad, 18 May 1963. In CONSTANT, *New Babylon*, Haags Gemeente-museum, The Hague, 1974.

Notes

[1] The operation *Grande Saison Dada* had been announced in the magazine Littéra-ture, 19, and was described the day following the visit in Comœdia of 15 April, in an article entitled *Les Disciples de DADA à l'Église Saint-Julien-le Pauvre*. The episode has been narrated by two of the participants: Andre Parinaud (ed.), *Andre Breton - Entretiens*, Gallimard, Paris 1952, and Georges Ribemont-Dessaignes, *Déjà jadis*, René Juillard, Paris 1958. For further discussion: Michel Sanouillet, *Dada à Paris*, Jean-Jacques Pauvert, 1965; Georges Hugnet, *L'Aventure Dada*, Galerie de l'Institut, Paris, 1957. With the first visit, other excursions in the center of Paris were announced to the "Places that do not truly have any reason to exist": the Louvre, the park of Buttes-Chaumont, the Gare Saint-Lazare, the Canal de l'Ourcq and Mont du Petit Cadenas (off the map). These excursions never took place, but they are described in the walks in the surrealistic novels of Louis Aragon and Andre Breton.

[2] André Parinaud, *André Breton...*, op. cit. p. 48.

[3] Here the reference is at the book *Le mouvement* by Etienne-Jules Marey edited in 1894 with the crono-photographic studies of human locomotion made in 1886. These are the photos that would inspire the *Nu descendant an escalier* of Duchamp and futuristic attempts to represent the dynamism of Balla's paintings and Boccioni's sculptures.

[4] On the theme of flânerie see: Walter Benjamin, *Die Wiederkher des Flâneurs*, in Franz Hessel, Spazieren in Berlin, 1929; Walter Benjamin, *Le Flâneur. Le Paris du Second Empire chez Baudelaire*, in Charles Baudelaire: *Ein Lyriker im Zeitalter des Hochkapitalismus*, Suhrkamp Verlag, Frankfurt am Main 1969 (English version: Charles Baudelaire: a Lyric Poet in the Era of High Capitalism, NLB, London 1973); Jean-Hubert Martin, *Dérives. Itineraires surréalistes, dérives et autres parcours*, in Cartes et cartographie de la Terre, Centre George Pompidou, Paris 1980. Christel Hollevoet, *Quand l'objet de l'art est la démarche, flânerie, dérive et autres deambulations*, in Exposé, 2, Orléans 1995; Christel Hollevoet, *Deambulation dans la ville, de*

la flânerie et la dérive a l'apprehension de l'espace urbain dans Fluxus et l'art conceptuel, in Parachute, 68, 1992 ; AA.VV., « Le visiteur » n°5, Printemps 2000; Rebecca Solnit, *Wanderlust. A history of walking*, Viking Penguin, 2000; Rebecca Solnit, *Walking and Thinking and Walking*, in "Kunstforum, Aestettik des Reisens", n° 136, 1997, pp.117-131; Thierry Davila, *Marcher Creer*, Editions du regard, Paris, 2002.

[5] The operation had been announced in the magazine *Littérature*, 19, and was described the day following the visit in *Comœdia* of 15 April, in an article entitled "Les Disciples de DADA à l'Église Saint-Julien-le-Pauvre". The episode has been narrated by two of the participants: André Parinaud (ed.), *André Breton - Entretiens*, Gallimard, Paris, 1952, and Georges Ribemont-Dessaignes, *Déjà jadis*, René Juillard, Paris, 1958. For further discussion: Michel Sanouillet, *Dada à Paris*, Jean-Jacques Pauvert, 1965; Georges Hugnet, *L'Aventure Dada*, Galerie de l'Institut, Paris, 1957.

[6] André Parinaud, *André Breton…*, op cit, pp. 53-54

[7] André Breton, *Manifeste du Surrealisme* (1924), in Manifestes du Surréalisme, Pauvert, Paris 1962.

[8] Louis Aragon, *Le paysan de Paris*, Gallimard, Paris 1926, p. 155. Deambulation continues throughout much of the Surrealist output. The exploration of the city had already begun in the Dada years, and the results of those first journeys had gradually found their way into the writings of the group. The books and stories written in those years are dense with urban walks, and they are also the only evidence remaining. Some of these experiences were gathered in the magazine Littérature, which contains the first pieces of automatic writing, the narrations of dreams, shared games like questionnaires, word games, verbal associations, the collective game-poems and the first experiences of wandering in real space. Among the most famous surrealistic erratic novels see: André Breton, *Les Pas Perdus*, Gallimard, Paris 1924; André Breton, *Nadja*, N.R.F., Paris 1928; Marcel Morise, *Itineraire du temps de la préhistoire à nos jours*, in «La révolution surréaliste» n°11, Paris 1928.

[9] Mirella Bandini, *La vertigine del moderno - percorsi surrealisti*, Officina Edizioni, Roma, 1986, p. 120. See also Mirella Bandini, *L'estetico il politico. Da Cobra all'Internazionale Situazionista 1948-1957*, Ed. Officina, Rome 1977.

[10] Andre Breton, *Pont Neuf*, in *La Clé des champs*, Paris 1953, cited in Mirella Bandini, *Surrealist References in the Notions of Dérive and Psycogeography of the Situationist Urban Environment*, in Libero Andreotti & Xavier Costa (eds.), *Situacionists: Art, Politics, Urbanism*, Museu d'Art Contemporani de Barcelona / Actar, Barcelona, 1996.

[11] The phrases are from issues 1 and 5 of "Potlatch", the International Lettrist Review completely reprinted in Gerard Berreby, *Documents relatifs à la fondation de l' Internationale Situationniste 1948-1957*, Ed. Alia, Paris, 1985.

[12] Ivan Chtcheglov alias Gilles Ivain, *Formulaire pour un Urbanisme Nouveau*, written in 1953 and edited in "I.S." n°1, p.15.

[13] Guy E. Debord, *Introduction a une critique de la géographie urbaine*, «Les Lèvres Nues» n° 6, pp. 11-15, Bruxelles, september 1955.

[14] All the quotes came from Guy E. Debord, *Théorie de la dérive*, in «Les Lèvres Nues», 8/9, Brussels, 1956. Republished in *"Internationale Situatiónniste"*, 2, De-

cember 1958; (English version: *Theory of the Dérive*, in Libero Andreotti and Xavier Costa (eds.), *Theory of the Dérive and Other Situatinist Writings on the City*, Museu D'Art Contemporany de Barcelona/ Actar, 1996. See also Simon Sadler, *The Situationist City*, Mit Press, Cambridge Mass. 1998.

[15] See Johan Huizinga, *Homo Ludens*, Amsterdam-Leipzig 1939.

[16] Constant, *Another City for Another Life*, "I.S." n°3, p. 37.

[17] On Alba and the Experimental Laboratory see: Mirella Bandini, *Pinot Gallizio e il Laboratorio Sperimentale d'Alba*, Galleria Civica di Arte Moderna, Torino 1974; Sandro Ricaldone, *Jorn in Italia. Gli anni del Bauhaus Immaginista*, Fratelli Pozzo, Moncalieri 1997; Giorgina Bertolino, Francesca Comisso and Maria Teresa Roberto, *Pinot Gallizio. Il laboratorio della scrittura*, Charta, Milano 2005; Francesco Careri, Armin Linke and Luca Vitone, *Constant e le radici di New Babylon*, "Domus" n° 885, october 2005. On the relationships with avangarde see: Reyner Banham, *Megastructure*, London 1976; Luigi Prestinenza Puglisi, *This is Tomorrow, avanguardie e architettura contemporanea*, Testo & Immagine, Torino 1999.

[18] Constant, *New Babylon*, Haags Gemeentemuseum, The Hague, 1974, reprinted in Jean Clarence Lambert, *New Babylon - Constant. Art et Utopie*, Cercle d'art, Paris 1997, p. 49. On New Babylon see also: Jean Clarence Lambert, *Constant. Les trois espaces*, cercle d'art, Paris 1992 ; Mark Wigley, *Constant's New Babylon. The Hyper-Architecture of Desire*, Witte de With Center for Contemporary Art / 010, Rotterdam 1998; Francesco Careri, *Constant / New Babylon, una città nomade*, Testo & Immagine, Torino 2001.

[19] See Guy E. Debord, *Unitary Urbanism at the End of the 1950s*, "I.S." n° 3, p. 11; Constant, Guy E. Debord, The Amsterdam declaration, "I.S." n° 2, p. 31; Constant et all., Rapporto inaugurale della Conferenza di Monaco, "I.S." n° 3, p. 26; Leonardo Lippolis, Urbanismo Unitario, Testo & Immagine, Torino 2002.

[20] Constant, "New Babylon - Ten Years On", lecture at the University of Delft, 23 May 1980, in Mark Wigley, *Constant's New Babylon. The Hyper-Architecture of Desire*, Witte de With Center for Contemporary Art of Rotterdam / 010, Rotterdam, 1998. p. 236.

[21] Giulio Carlo Argan, *L'arte moderna 1770-1970*, Sansoni, Firenze 1970, p. 431.

[22] Constant, *New Babylon...*, op cit., p. 30.

"I chose to make art by walking, utilizing lines and circles, or stones and days."
Richard Long

"My art form is the short journey made by walking in the landscape. [...] The only thing we should take of a landscape are photographs. The only thing we should leave are footprints."
Hamish Fulton

"Walking conditioned sight, and sight conditioned walking, till it seemed only the feet could see."
Robert Smithson

Land Walk

The Voyage of Tony Smith

In December 1966 the magazine *Artforum* published the story of a journey by Tony Smith along a highway under construction on the outskirts of New York. Gilles Tiberghien considers this experience of the New Jersey Turnpike lived by Tony Smith—seen by many as the "father" of American Minimal Art—to be the origin of Land Art, and the predecessor of an entire series of walks in deserts and the urban peripheries that took place in the late 1960s.[1]

One evening, with some students at Cooper Union, Smith decided to sneak into the Turnpike construction site and to drive down the black ribbon of asphalt that crosses the marginal spaces of the American periphery like an empty gash. During the trip Smith feels a sort of ineffable ecstasy he defines as "the end of art" and wonders, "The road and much of the landscape was artificial, and yet it couldn't be called a work of art."[2] This went straight to the heart of a basic problem regarding the aesthetic nature of the path: can the road be considered an artwork? If it can, in what way? As a large readymade? As an abstract sign crossing the landscape? As an object or as an experience? As a space in its own right or as an act of crossing? What is the role of the surrounding landscape?

The story leads to many questions and many possible paths of investigation. The road is seen by Tony Smith in the two different possible ways that were to be analyzed by Minimal Art and Land

The End of Art "When I was teaching at Cooper Union in the first year or two of the fifties, someone told me how I could get onto the unfinished New Jersey Turnpike. I took three students and drove from some-where in the Meadows to New Brunswick. It was a dark night and there were no lights or shoulder markers, lines, railings, or anything at all except the dark pavement moving through the landscape of the flats, rimmed by hills in the distance, but punctuated by stacks, towers, fumes, and colored lights. This drive was a revealing experience. The road and much of the landscape was artificial, and yet it couldn't be called a work of art. On the other hand, it did something for me that art had never done. At first, I didn't know what it was, but its effect was to liberate me from many of the views I had had about art. It seemed that there had been a reality there that had not had any expression in art.

The experience on the road was something mapped out but not socially recognized. I thought to myself, it ought to be clear that's the end of art. Most painting looks pretty pictorial after that. There is no way you can frame it, you just have to experience it. Later I discovered some abandoned airstrips in Europe–abandoned works, Surrealist landscapes, something that had nothing to do with any function, created worlds without tradition. Artificial landscape without cultural precedent began to dawn on me. There is a drill ground in Nuremberg, large enough to accommodate two million men. The entire field is enclosed with high embankments and towers. The concrete approach is three sixteen-inch steps, one above the other, stretching for a mile or so."

S. Wagstaff, "Talking with Tony Smith", in *Artforum*, December 1966.

Regarding the terms of the debate that developed in *Artforum* and an in-depth study of the art scene at the time, cf. GILLES A. TIBERGHIEN, *Land Art*, Carré, Paris, 1993, (English version: *Land Art*, Princeton Architectural Press, New York, 1995). ROSALIND KRAUSS, *Passages in Modern Sculpture*, MIT Press, Cambridge, MA, 1981.

Art and Objecthood

"What seems to have been revealed to Smith that night was the pictorial nature of painting—even, one might say, the conventional nature of art. And this Smith seems to have understood not as laying bare the essence of art, but as announcing its end. In comparison with the unmarked, unlit, all but unstructured turnpike—more precisely, with the turnpike as experienced from within the car, traveling on it—art appears to have struck Smith as almost absurdly small. [...] The experience is clearly regarded by Smith as wholly accessible to everyone, not just in principle but in fact, and the question of whether or not one has really had it does not arise. [...] But what was Smith's experience on the turnpike? Or to put the same question another way, if the turnpike, airstrips, and drill ground are not works of art, what are they?—What, indeed, if not empty, or 'abandoned', situations? And what was Smith's experience if not the experience of what I have been calling theater? It is as though the turnpike, airstrips, and drill ground reveal the theatrical character of literalist art, only without the object, that is, without the art itself—as though the object is needed only within a room (or, perhaps, in any circumstances less extreme than these). In each of the above cases the object is, so to speak, replaced by something: for example, on the turnpike by the constant onrush of the road, the simultaneous recession of new reaches of dark pavement illumined by the onrushing headlights, the sense of the turnpike itself as something enormous, abandoned, derelict, existing for Smith alone and for those in the car with him. [...]

Smith's account of his experience on the turnpike bears witness to theater's profound hostility to the arts, and discloses, precisely in the absence of the object and in what takes its place, what might be called the theatricality of objecthood. By the same token, however, the imperative that modernist painting defeat or suspend its object-hood is at bottom the imperative that it defeat or suspend theater. And this means that there is a war going on between theater and modernist painting, between the theatrical and the pictorial—a war that, despite the literalists' explicit rejection of modernist painting and sculpture, is not basically a matter of program and ideology but of experience, conviction, sensibility."

MICHAEL FRIED, "Art and Objecthood", in *Artforum*, June 1967.

Art: one is the road as sign and object, on which the crossing takes place; the other is the crossing itself as experience, as *attitude that becomes form.*[3]

This was not, in fact, the end of art, but a sudden intuition that was shortly thereafter to take art out of the galleries and museums to reclaim the experience of lived space and the larger scale of the landscape. Although the experience of Tony Smith still seems quite similar to the Dada readymade, from this moment on the practice of walking begins to be transformed into a true autonomous artform. What seemed like an aesthetic realization, an immediate flash of intuition, an almost indescribable ecstasy, is then utilized in countless ways by a great number of artists—most of them sculptors—who emerged at the end of the 1960s in a passage from Minimalism to that series of very heterogeneous experiences categorized under the generic term of 'Land Art.' This passage is easily understood if we compare the works of Carl Andre with those of Richard Long, two artists who seem to have taken the experience of Tony Smith in two different directions.

In his process of the canceling or reduction of sculpture, Carl Andre tried to make objects that could occupy space without filling it, to create *presences* that were increasingly *absent* within real space. His goal was very similar to the long black road of Tony Smith: a sort of infinite carpet, a two-dimensional space to inhabit, an abstract ground, artificial, dilated, prolonged and flattened like a foundation without thickness, on which no sculpture rests, but simultaneously defining a space that is experienced by the observer.

To clarify the subsequent passage from the minimal object to the objectless experience, we can turn to two interviews with Carl Andre and Richard Long. Andre states, "Actually, for me the ideal sculpture is a road. [...] Most of my works, in any case the best ones, are somehow roads—they require you to follow them, to walk around them or go onto them."[4] Richard Long responds,

> What distinguishes his work from mine is that he has
> made flat sculptures on which we can walk. It's a space
> on which to walk that can be moved and put somewhere

Walkscapes – walking as an aesthetic practice

else, while my art consists in the act of walking itself. Carl Andre makes objects on which to walk, my art is made by walking. This is a fundamental difference.[5]

Therefore Smith's perplexities seem, just a few years later, to have already found resolutions in two directions: for Andre the road experienced by Smith is not only art, it is the ideal sculpture; Long goes further, saying that art consists in the very act of walking, of living the experience. At this point it seems clear that the fundamental step has been taken. With Long the passage has been made from the object to its absence. The erratic path returns to its status as an aesthetic form in the field of the visual arts.

The first attempts to use walking as an art form—or, more precisely, as a form of anti-art—were made as an expansion of the field of action of literature into the visual arts. The collective forms of the visit, the deambulation and the *dérive,* in fact, were experiences born in a literary sphere, and the connection linking Tristan Tzara, André Breton, and Guy Debord is a literary one. In the 1960s the consequences of their research were explored by artists interested in the theatrical space of performance art and urban happenings with Dada roots, but also by sculptors with a focus on the space of architecture and the landscape. The return to walking in the field of sculpture is an integral part of a more general expansion of sculpture itself. The artists take steps that seem to trace back through all the stages that led from the erratic journey to the menhir, and the menhir to architecture. In their works we can once again see a logical thread that goes from minimal objects (the menhir), to the territorial works of Land Art (the landscape) and the wanderings of the Land artists (walking). A thread that connects walking to that field of activity that operates as transformation of the earth's surface, a field of action shared by architecture and landscape design. To effect this passage it is again necessary to find an empty field of action, in which the signs of history and civilization are absent: the deserts and the *terrain vague* of the abandoned urban periphery.

RICHARD LONG, Walking a Line in Peru, 1972.

CARL ANDRE, *Sixteen Steel Cardinals*, 1974.

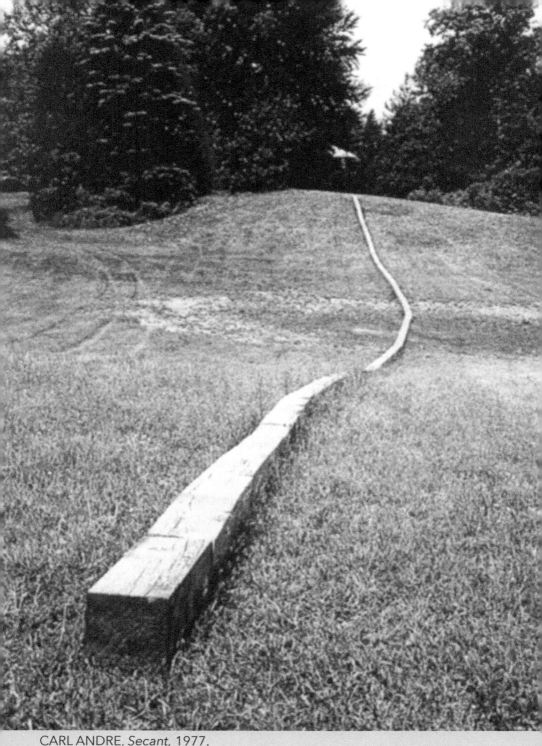

CARL ANDRE, *Secant*, 1977.

Field Expansions

In June 1967 the critic Michael Fried, prompted by Tony Smith's tale, responded in the pages of *Artforum* with an article entitled "Art and Objecthood," in which Smith's experience is seen as a clear example of the war being waged by theater and literature against art.[6] Fried was concerned about the growing invasion of other arts in the field of sculpture and painting, and called for a return of all the arts within their own disciplinary boundaries. The enemy was that experimentalism which, as we have seen, had been christened *urbanisme unitaire* by the Situationists, and which tended, under different names, to move in the direction of a sort of unifying interdisciplinary approach. Actually, unitary urbanism had never been realized, and sculpture had not trespassed beyond its own disciplinary confines; it was simply trying to come to grips with its own limits, to work on its margins to enlarge its field of action. Rather than being invaded by theatrical space, sculpture was invading, with increasingly awareness, the *living space life*, and therefore the theater, dance, architecture, and landscape.

In homage to *Arena Quad I+II* of Samuel Beckett and the character Molloy, Bruce Nauman walked for about an hour on a space defined by starting with a line drawn on the ground. With his hands clasped behind his back, placing one leg at a time on the ground, walking—instead of an ordinary gesture—becomes a dance of the weights and continuous re-balancing of the body while giving rise, through the sound of the cadenced steps, to a rhythmical, sonorous space.

According to Rosalind Krauss, sculpture after the 1950s was experienced as the negative of architecture and landscape: "That which, on top of or in front of a building, was not a building; or that which, inserted in a landscape, was not a landscape. [...] At this point it was the category resulting from non-landscape and non-architecture. [...] But non-architecture is simply another form of definition of the landscape, and non-landscape is, to put it more simply, architecture."[7] Utilizing a system of mathematical expansion, Rosalind Krauss thus graphically expresses the *expanded field* in which sculpture operates after the 1960s: below we find modernist sculpture derived from the pairing non-architecture and non-landscape, while above, the two pos-

Walkscapes – walking as an aesthetic practice

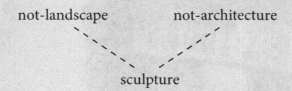

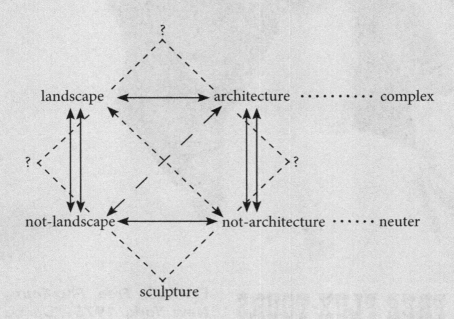

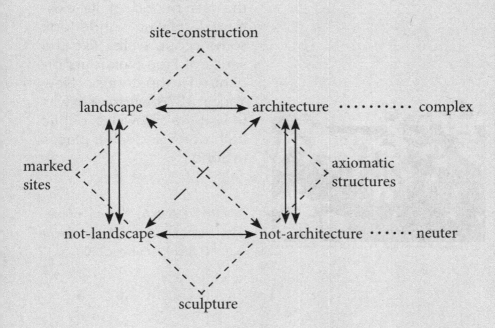

FREE FLUX-TOURS

(EXCEPT FOR COST OF TRANSPORTATION & MEALS IF ANY)

May 1: MAYDAY, guided by Bob Watts, call 226-3422 for transportation arrangements.
May 3: FRANCO AMERICAN TOUR, by Alison Knowles & Robert Filliou, 2 pm at 80 Wooster st
May 4: TOUR FOR FOREIGN VISITORS, arranged by George Brecht, start noon at 80 Wooster st
May 5: ALLEYS, YARDS & DEAD ENDS, arranged by G. Maciunas, start 3 pm at 80 Wooster st.
May 6: ALEATORIC TOUR, arranged by James Riddle, meet at noon at 80 Wooster st
May 7: MUSIC TOUR & LECTURE, by Yoshimasa Wada, start at 2 pm at 80 Wooster st
May 8: GALLERIES, guided by Larry Miller, start at noon at 80 Wooster st.
May 9: SUBTERRANEAN TOUR I, guided by Geoff Hendricks, start at noon at 80 Wooster st
May 9: SUBTERRANEAN DANGER, by Charles Bergengren, start 11 am at 47st. & Park av, 30 and
May 10 & 11: at 6 am go to 17 Mott street and eat Wonton soup from Nam Jone Park?
May 12: SUBTERRANEAN TOUR III, arranged by George Maciunas, start 2 pm at 80 Wooster st.
May 13: SOUVENIR HUNT, meet at noon at 80 Wooster st
May 14: SOHO CURB SITES, guided by Peter Van Riiper, meet at 3.30 pm at 80 Wooster st
May 15: EXOTIC SITES, guided by Jean Mathews, meet 3 pm at Ocindu Restaurant, 202/6-14 st.
May 16: ALL THE WAY AROUND & BACK AGAIN, by Peter Frank, meet at noon 80 Wooster

GEORGE MACIUNAS ET AL., «FREE FLUX TOURS», MAI 1976

FLUXUS, *Free Flux-Tours*, New York, 1976. "During the last period of its existence, Fluxus undertook some group walks, like the series of Free Flux-Tours organized in the streets of New York in 1976, whose aim was to visit the sidewalks, public bathrooms and other places in Soho."

THIERRY DAVILA, "Errare humanum est", in *Les Figures de la marche*, RNM, Antibes, 2000.

BRUCE NAUMAN, *Slow Angle Walk* (Beckett
Walk), 1968.

itive elements of landscape and architecture identify the space of action of the *construction of places,* a space containing "labyrinths, mazes, Japanese gardens, places for games and for ritual processions."[8] Therefore it is necessary to reconsider sculpture in a wider historical framework, one "undertaking the construction of its genealogies, starting with data that no longer date back mere decades, but millennia."[9]

Gilles Tiberghien heads in the direction indicated by Krauss, in an attempt to return to the most elementary categories:

> If the history of the relations between architecture and sculpture is complex, and involves, as Hegel says, a sort of *division of functions,* it would appear that for a certain number of sculptures of Land Art what is at stake is a return to the very origins of this history.[10]

The division of functions is that in which architecture has the function of a place of shelter, or worship or gathering, while sculpture has the function of presenting the image of man or of god. Hegel, in his *Lectures on Aesthetics,* says that the origins of sculpture and architecture "should have an immediate, simple character, and not the relativity that comes from the division of the functions. Our force therefore is to seek a point situated beyond this division." Considering architecture in its exclusively symbolic function, Hegel looks not for works of architecture that immediately translate an internal meaning in the external form, but works whose meaning must be sought elsewhere, like symbols. This type of work that is independent of function, simultaneously sculpture and architecture, is defined by Hegel as "inorganic sculpture (*unorganische Skulptur*), because [these works] realize a symbolic form destined only to suggest or reawaken a representation." According to Hegel the first works of such non-functional and non-mimetic architecture are the Egyptian obelisks, colossal statues and the pyramids:

> It is only in inorganic creation that man is fully nature's equal, and creates driven by a profound desire and without an external model; when man crosses this borderline and

begins to create organic works, he becomes dependent on them, his creation loses any autonomy and becomes mere *imitation of nature.*

Tiberghien clarifies this concept by adding his own definition of inorganic sculpture to Hegel's definition: "A pure presentation of itself, the gift of naked presence," a characteristic found in certain works of Minimal and Land Art that are simultaneously sculpture and architecture, and that approach the territory as large abstract forms, free of any imitative tendency.

According to Tiberghien:

> Everything happened as if the Minimal artists, having wanted to restore a maximum of autonomy to sculpture, had rediscovered and given value to a certain number of elements sculpture shares with architecture, thanks to which it becomes possible to return to a sort of original form.

Many of the works of Land Art are situated, according to Tiberghien, "in advance of symbolism itself, in that sphere of non-separation of architecture and sculpture that corresponds to what Hegel calls the *primitive need of art.*"

At this point it seems useful to take another step backward with respect to Hegel, and to look at the menhir as an archetype of inorganic sculpture. Following this backtracking logic, the path can be seen as belonging to that sphere situated beyond the inorganic sculpture Hegel calls "the primitive need of art," and Rosalind Krauss calls "the construction of places." Considering architecture, too, as a discipline that operates in its own expanded field, we should expect to find sculpture, landscape, and path within it. Their common field of action is the activity of symbolic transformation of the territory. Walking, therefore, is situated in a sphere where it is still simultaneously sculpture, architecture, and landscape, between the *primitive need of art* and *inorganic sculpture.*

The obelisk and the pyramid cited by Hegel as the first inorganic sculptures descend from the *benben* and the menhir, which in turn descend from wandering. Thus we can view the menhir as the first inorganic sculpture, a symbolic, non-mimetic form that carries inside it the home and the image of God, the column that was to give rise to architecture, and the statue that was to give rise to sculpture. But the menhir is also the first symbolic construction of the Earth's surface that transforms the landscape from a natural to an artificial state. Therefore the menhir contains architecture, sculpture, and landscape. Thus we can understand why Minimal sculpture, in order to re-appropriate architectonic space, had to go back to come to terms with the menhir, in order to then evolve in the direction of Land Art. And in this journey back to and from the menhir, the path suddenly reappears, seen this time as *sculpture in an expanded field*, and no longer as a literary form.

In the attempt to annul everything that until that point had been considered sculpture, the Minimal artists found themselves at a sort of *ground zero* of their discipline. In this process of subtraction they had found objects extraneous to nature, contrasting the natural landscape by means of the artificial signs of culture, erasing that sort of animated presence that had always lurked inside sculpture. The artists had undertaken a series of passages that led them back to the menhir: the elimination of the base or pedestal to return to a direct relationship with the sky and the ground (the menhir is directly planted in the ground); the return to the monolith and the mass (the three parts of the column in architecture corresponded, in sculpture, to the subdivisions of the totem); the elimination of color and natural materials in favor of artificial, industrial materials, artifacts (the stone of the menhir was, in the Stone Age, the most 'artificial' material found in nature, and its vertical position was the least natural imaginable); compositions based on simple, rhythmical, and serial repetition (points, lines, surfaces); elimination of any adjectival impulses in favor of pure, crystalline forms; removal of the figurative mimesis that still existed in zoomorphic, anthropomorphic, and totemic modern sculptures; recovery of a sort of human dimension and therefore of a more abstract, theatrical anthropomorphism due to that residual "animated presence" that continues to persist in sculpture.

The result of these operations is a monomateric, situated, fixed, immobile, inert, inexpressive, almost dead object. But it is an object

Walkscapes – walking as an aesthetic practice

that imposes a certain distance and has a new relationship with its space; it is a character without internal life but, at the same time, it takes possession of the space, forcing the observer to participate, to share an experience that goes beyond the visible and that addresses, like architecture, the entire body, its presence in time and space.

From the Menhir to the Path

While the Minimal object moves toward the menhir, still seen as an object with an internal presence, Land Art moves, instead, more directly toward architecture and landscape, i.e. toward the menhir as an inanimate object to be utilized to transform the territory. Starting in 1966, the year of the publication of Tony Smith's journey, sculpture rapidly regained the ground taken from it by architecture; ground not only in the sense of disciplinary territory, but also of physical terrain, large portions of the Earth's surface. Sculptors laid claim to new spaces, in the belief that sculpture had a right to take part in that action of transformation and modeling of the signs and materials of the territory from which it had been excluded since the Neolithic period, since sculpture had been subjugated to architectural space as the totem at the center of the village, the image on the fronton of a temple, a work in a museum or a statue in the park. The objective of Land Art is no longer the modeling of large or small objects in open space, but the physical transformation of the territory, the use of the means and techniques of architecture to construct a new nature and to create large artificial landscapes. Any sculptural anthropomorphism still surviving in Minimalist sculptures is abandoned in favor of that even more abstract mimesis that characterizes architecture and landscape.

The surface of the Earth, over the course of the millennia, has been engraved, designed, and constructed by architecture, incessantly superimposing a system of cultural signs on a system of original, natural signs; the Earth of the Land artists is sculpted, drawn on, cut, excavated, disrupted, packaged, lived, and crossed anew through the archetypal signs of human thought. In Land Art we can see a conscious *return to the Neolithic.*[11] Long rows of stones planted in the ground, fences of leaves or branches, spirals of earth, lines and circles designed on the ground, or enormous excavations of the terrain, large monuments in earth, cement, iron and formless pourings of industrial materials are utilized as means of appropriation of space, as primal actions toward an archaic nature, as anthropic intervention in a primitive landscape. The spaces in which these operations take place are spaces without architecture or signs of human presence, *empty* spaces in which to realize works that take on the meaning of a primordial sign, a unique trace in an archaic, atemporal landscape. All this seems almost like a desire to start all over again from the beginning of the history of the world, to go back to point zero in order to find a unitary discipline, in which the art of the Earth—and in this sense the term 'earthwork' used by Smithson seems much more convincing than the term Land Art—was the only means available with which to come to grips with natural space and infinite time.

We will not linger here over an analysis of the major works built by the Land artists, just as we did not delve into the works of architecture after those of the Egyptians. These works are incredible spaces to walk through, but they would open up another field of investigation, too vast and too closely connected to architecture itself.

Instead, we will attempt to understand how some of the Land artists rediscovered walking as a primary act of symbolic transformation of the territory. An action that is not a physical transformation of the territory, but a crossing of it that doesn't need to leave permanent traces, that acts only superficially on the world, but can achieve proportions even greater than those of the earthworks.

Treading the World

In 1967, the year after the publication of the journey of Tony Smith, on the other side of the Atlantic, Richard Long produced *A Line Made by Walking*, a straight line 'sculpted' on the ground simply by treading on grass. The result of this action is a sign that remains only on photographic film, disappearing from the ground when the grass returns to its original position. *A Line Made by Walking*, thanks to its radical clarity and formal simplicity, is considered a fundamen-

Richard Long, *A Line Made by Walking*, 1967

tal point of passage in contemporary art. Rudi Fuchs has compared it to the black square of Kasimir Malevich, "a fundamental interruption of the history of art."[12]

Guy Tosatto considers it "one of the most singular and revolutionary gestures of 20th-century sculpture,"[13] and Hamish Fulton, the English artist who has often accompanied Richard Long in his continental wanderings, interpreting the art of walking in keeping with his own expressive forms, sees this first work by Long as

> one of the most original works of occidental art in the 20th century. (The long journey begins with a single step.) When he was only 23 years old Long combined two apparently separate activities: sculpture (the line) and walking (the action). *A line (made by) walking.* In time the sculpture would disappear.[14]

The infinite line of black asphalt on which the ecstasy of Smith begins to take form, avoiding its transformation into an object.

A Line Made by Walking produces a sensation of infinity, it is a long segment that stops at the trees that enclose the visual field, but could continue around the entire planet. The image of the treaded grass contains the presence of absence: absence of action, absence of the body, absence of the object. But it is also unmistakably the result of the action of a body, and it is an object, a something that is situated between sculpture, a performance, and an architecture of the landscape. The later works of Long and Fulton are the continuation and embellishment of this initial gesture, of which no trace has remained on the ground itself. The basis for the works of Long and Fulton is walking, the setting in which the works take place is a natural, timeless space, an eternally primordial landscape where the presence of the artist is already a symbolic act in itself.[15]

Fulton develops the theme of walking as an act of celebration of the uncontaminated landscape, a sort of ritual pilgrimage through what remains of nature. His work involves environmental and ecological concerns, and his journeys can also be interpreted as a form of protest: "My work can evidently be inserted in the history of art,

Walkscapes – walking as an aesthetic practice

but never in the past has there been an era in which my concerns had such significance as today. [...] The open spaces are disappearing. [...] For me being in nature is a form of immediate religion."[16] Long acknowledges that "nature produces much more effect on me than I do on her."[17] For the two artists nature corresponds to an inviolable Mother Earth on which one can walk, design figures, move stones, but without effecting any radical transformation. This is the factor that has led to their repeated dissent regarding the Land artists. The roots of their research go back to the culture of the Celtic megalith, far from the massive transformation of American landscapes. For Long, "Land Art is an American expression. It means bulldozers and big projects. To me it seems like a typically American movement; it is the construction of works on land purchased by the artists with the aim of making a large, permanent monument. All this absolutely does not interest me."[18] Long's intervention is free of any technological aid, it doesn't cut into the Earth's crust, but merely transforms the surface in a reversible way. The only means utilized is his own body, his possibility of movement, the strength of his arms and legs: the largest stone utilized is one that can be moved by a single person, and the longest path is the one the body can follow in a certain period of time. The body is a tool for measuring space and time. Through the body Long measures his own perceptions and the variations in atmospheric agents, he uses walking to capture the changes in the direction of the winds, in temperature and sounds. To measure means identifying points, indicating them, aligning them, circumscribing spaces, alternating them in keeping with a rhythm and a direction, and here again Long's work has primordial roots: geometry as the *measure of the world.*[19]

The Wayfarer on the Map

One of the main problems of the art of walking is the communication of the experience in aesthetic form. The Dadaists and Surrealists did not transfer their actions onto a cartographic base, and avoided representation by resorting to literary description; the Situationists produced their psychogeographic maps, but did not want

RICHARD LONG, Dartmoor Riverbeds. A Four-Day Walk Along All the Riverbeds Within a Circle on Dartmoor, 1978

A series of tours made inside a circle drawn on a plan, following all the banks of the rivers and streams within that circle. "In *Circle of Crossing Places* the idea was to make a circular walk on Dartmoor and just record all the rivers and streams and brooks that I crossed. It was the naming of the watery places. It was a sort of watery walk as a perfect circle. In *Dartmoor Riverbeds* I used all the riverbeds as footpaths, within a large imaginary circle."

RICHARD LONG, A Six-Day Walk Over All Roads, Lanes and Double Tracks inside a Six-Mile-Wide Circle Centered on The Giant of Cerne Abbas, 1975.

Cartography, Narrative, Journey

"The simplest form of a geographical map is not the one that seems most natural to us today, or namely a map representing the surface of the ground as seen by an extraterrestrial gaze.

The first need to put places on a map is connected with travel: it is the reminder of the succession of the stages, the tracing of a route.

[...]

Following a path from the beginning to the end gives a special kind of satisfaction, both in life and in literature (the journey as narrative structure), so one may well wonder why the theme of the journey has not met with the same success, and only appears sporadically, in the figurative arts.

[...]

The need to comprehend in one image both the dimension of time and that of space lies at the origin of cartography. Time as a story of the past [...] and time in the future: as the presence of obstacles that are encountered on the journey, and here the weather (*tempo atmosferico*) is joined with chronological time (*tempo cronologico*).

[...]

The geographical map, in short, although static, implies a narrative idea, it is conceived in keeping with an itinerary, it is an Odyssey."

ITALO CALVINO, Il Viandante Nella Mappa, 1984

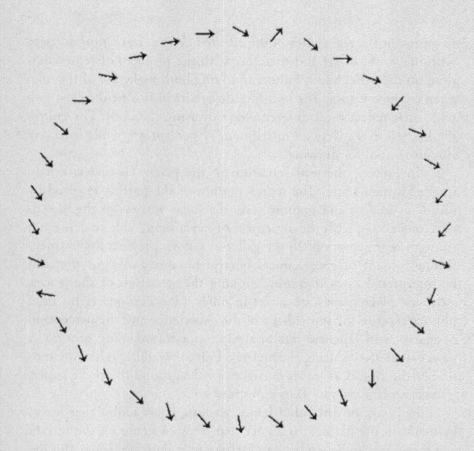

RICHARD LONG, Dartmoor Wind Circle, 1985.

"That was very much to do with the fact that not only does the wind blow from a prevailing part of the sky, but it also reflects the shape of the land. When you walk over a ridge you get the wind blowing at you from the opposite direction, because it's being sucked up over the ridge. Then sometimes, if you go behind a big boulder or a tor, the wind can be deflected in another direction because of it. So wind can blow in all different directions for different reasons to do with the shape of the land. I very much liked the idea that in a subtle way the wind line was also reflecting the shape of the land."
ANNE SEYMOUR, *Richard Long: Walking in Circles*, G. Braziller, New York, 1991.

to represent the real routes of the effected *dérives*. In coming to grips with the world of art and therefore with the problem of representation, on the other hand, Fulton and Long both make use of the map as an expressive tool. The two English artists in this field follow two paths that reflect their different ways of using the body. For Fulton the body is exclusively an instrument of perception, while for Long it is also a tool for drawing.

In Fulton, the representation of the places crossed is a map in the abstract sense. The representation of the path is resolved by means of images and graphic texts that bear witness to the experience of walking with the awareness of never being able to achieve it through representation. In the galleries Fulton presents his journeys through a sort of geographical poetry: phrases and signs that can be interpreted as cartography, evoking the sensation of the places, altitudes, place names, distances in miles. Like Zen poetry his brief phrases capture the immediacy of the experience and the perception of space, as in Japanese haiku, aiming at a reawakening of a *hic et nunc* experienced during the journey. Fulton's walking is like the motion of the clouds, it leaves no traces on the ground or on the paper: "Walks are like clouds. They come and go."[20]

In Long, on the other hand, walking is an action that leaves its mark on the place. It is an act that draws a figure on the terrain and therefore can be reported in cartographic representation. But the procedure can be utilized in an inverse sense, the paper can function as a surface on which to draw figures to be subsequently walked: once a circle has been drawn on a map, you can cross its diameter, walk its edge, walk outside it... Long utilizes cartography as a base on which to plan his itineraries, and the choice of the territory in which to walk is related to the selected figure. Here walking is not only an action, it is also a sign, a form that can be superimposed on existing forms, both in reality and on paper.

Thus the world becomes an immense aesthetic territory, an enormous canvas on which to draw by walking. A surface that is not a white page, but an intricate design of historical and geographical sedimentation on which to simply add one more layer. Walking the figures superimposed on the map-territory, the body of the wayfarer

134   *Walkscapes – walking as an aesthetic practice*

"Using a stone for a pillow, I drift towards the clouds."

SANTOKA TANEDA, *Haiku*. Between 1926 and 1940 Taneda had walked 28,000 miles.

"Walks are like clouds, They come and go."

HAMISH FULTON

BRIGHT LIGHTS OF THE CITY

A GLASS OF WATER

MIDDLE OF THE NIGHT IN THE DEPTHS OF WINTER AT THE BOTTOM OF A RIVER – FISH ARE SWIMMING ......?

ALL CONTEMPORARY ART IS URBAN ART – THERE ARE NO WORDS IN NATURE

From the summer of 1969 to the present day I have made only art resulting from the experience of walking in the landscape. Walking is the constant – the art medium is the variable.

WHO *DESIGNED* THESE CLOUDS?   WHO *INVENTED* THIS WATER?

As a 'walking artist' I have attempted to link the two separate worlds of contemporary art (economics, competition, storage, transportation) and walking (Nature, influence from First Nation Peoples, trekking – 'leave no trace', perceptions from physical activity… meditative slowness). On my walks: I do not directly rearrange, remove, sell and not return any elements of the natural environment. My artworks = control. My walks = freedom.

**WALKS ARE LIKE CLOUDS
THEY COME AND GO**

THE LIGHT OF DAY AND THE DARKNESS OF NIGHT

HAMISH FULTON, *Walking Beside the River Vechte*, Stadtische Galerie, Nordhorn, 1997.

The Punctuated Landscape

"Tony Smith writes about 'a dark pavement' that is 'punctuated by stacks, towers, fumes and colored lights.' (*Artforum*, December 1966.) The key word is 'punctuated'. In a sense, the 'dark pavement' could be considered a 'vast sentence', and the things perceived along it, 'punctuation marks'. '. . . tower . . . = the exclamation mark (!)'. '. . . stacks . . . = the dash (–)'. '. . . fumes . . . = the question mark (?)'. '. . . colored lights . . . = the colon (:)'. Of course, I form these equations on the basis of sense-data and not rational-data. Punctuation refers to interruptions in 'printed matter'. It is used to emphasize and clarify the meaning of specific segments of usage. Sentences like 'skylines' are made of separate 'things' that constitute a whole syntax. Tony Smith also refers to his art as 'interruptions' in a 'space-grid'. "

ROBERT SMITHSON, "Towards the Development of an Air Terminal Site", in *Artforum*, June 1967, reprinted in FLAM, JACK (ed.), *The Collected Writings, op. cit.*

Gilles Tiberghien reminds us of a predecessor of this type of landscape-sentence in the description of an English park by 'Capability' Brown reported in 1782 by Hannah More: "He said he compared his art to a literary composition: 'There–he said, pointing a finger–I make a comma, and there–pointing to another place–a colon, because a more decisive bend is necessary; in another place, where an interruption is needed to break up the visual continuity, there will be a parenthesis; then a full stop, and then I begin to make another sentence."

GILLES A. TIBERGHIEN, *Land Art, op. cit.*

registers the events of the journey, the sensations, obstacles, dangers, the variations of the terrain. The physical structure of the territory is reflected on the body in motion.[21]

The Suburban Odyssey

In the October 1967 issue of *Artforum* a letter to the editor responds ironically to the article by Michael Fried. It is signed by Robert Smithson, a young artist on the New York Minimalist scene, and the text is cutting and paradoxical. It is the

> prologue of a spectacular film not yet written, whose title is *The Tribulations of Michael Fried*. [...] Fried, the orthodox modernist, guardian of the gospels of Clement Greenberg, has been abducted in ecstasy by Tony Smith, *the agent of the infinite*. [...] He is gripped by terror of the infinite. The corruption of appearances of the infinite is worse than any known form of the Devil. A radical skepticism, known only to the terrible 'literalists', threatens the innermost essence of form. The labyrinths of an endless time—the virus of eternity—contaminate his brain. Fried, the holy Marxist, won't let himself be tempted by this perilous sensibility.[22]

One year after its publication, the voyage of Tony Smith remains at the center of the controversy between modernists and Minimalists.

Robert Smithson had already dealt with the issues raised by Tony Smith in the article "Toward the Development of an Air Terminal Site" in the June issue of *Artforum,* the same issue containing the article by Michael Fried. Smithson writes of "remote places like the Pine Barrens in New Jersey or the frozen plains of the North Pole and the South Pole, that can be reconsidered by forms of art that could use *the actual territory as a medium*."[23] He compares Tony Smith's road to the structure of a sentence that unwinds along the New Jersey Turnpike: the actual territory is a surreal medium through which we can read and write on space like a text. Naturalism "is replaced by a non-objective

IL PERSON ENTERS PRIVATE PLACE

VITO ACCONCI, Following Pieces, 1969

In 1969 Yoko Ono made the film *Rape* in London, randomly selecting a woman and following her with the camera for ten days through her urban itineraries. The same type of "stalking" was performed in New York by Vito Acconci (*Following Piece*, 1969), by Sophie Calle, who had her mother hire a private detective to tail her (*Detective*, 1981), and is also found in the novels of Paul Auster (*City of Glass*, 1985).

TWO LINES   THREE CIRCLES
ON THE DESERT

WALTER DE MARIA, Two Lines, Three Circles on the Desert, 1968

In 1968 Walter De Maria made his *One Mile Long Drawing*, two parallel one-mile lines drawn on the Mojave Desert, where in 1969 he shot, for the television gallery of Gerry Schum, the video *Two Lines, Three Circles on the Desert*: the artist walks in a straight line until he vanishes from the frame, while the camera completes three full pans.

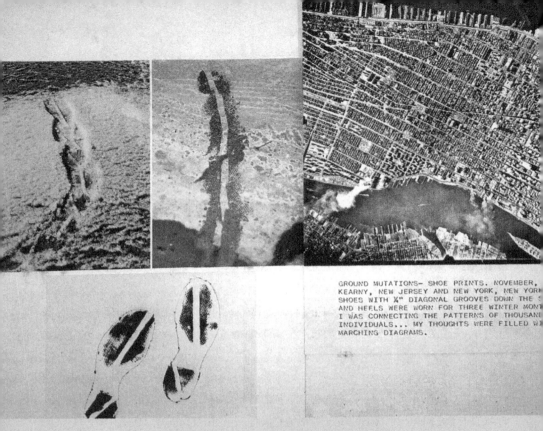

GROUND MUTATIONS– SHOE PRINTS. NOVEMBER,
KEARNY, NEW JERSEY AND NEW YORK, NEW YORK
SHOES WITH ¼" DIAGONAL GROOVES DOWN THE S
AND HEELS WERE WORN FOR THREE WINTER MONT
I WAS CONNECTING THE PATTERNS OF THOUSAN
INDIVIDUALS... MY THOUGHTS WERE FILLED WI
MARCHING DIAGRAMS.

In November 1969 Dennis Oppenheim made *Ground Mutation-Shoe Prints*, a work consisting in leaving footprints on the ground. For three months Oppenheim wore a pair of shoes he had modified with six-millimeter cuts on the sole and heel: "I wanted to connect all the footprints of thousands of individuals. [...] My thoughts were completely occupied by diagrams of paths."

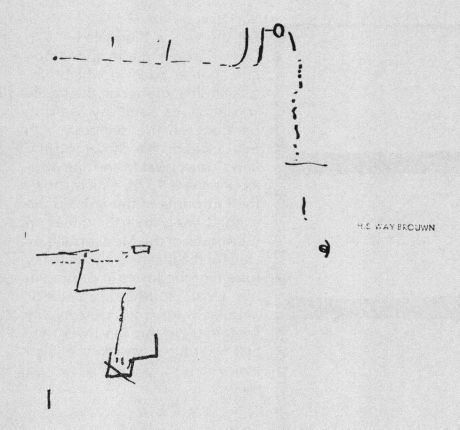

H.S WAY BROUWN

THIS WAY BROUWN

On 25-26 February 1961 in Amsterdam Stanley Brouwn asked randomly selected passersby to draw him, on different sheets of paper, directions to reach another point in the city. "As they were drawing the people talked, and at times they talked more than they drew. On the sketches we can see what the people were explaining. But we cannot see what they have omitted, because they had trouble realizing that what might be clear to them still requires explanation." STANLEY BROUWN, *This Way Brouwn*, 25-2-61, Verlag Gebr. König, Köln/New York, 1961.

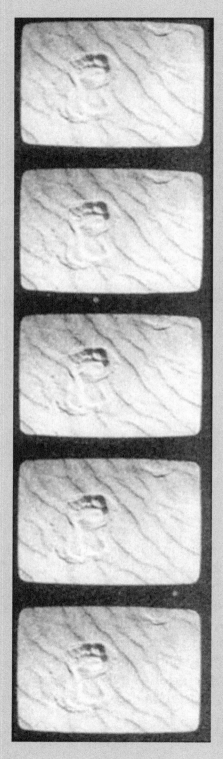

For the Venice Biennale in 1976 Dani Karavan made the *Ambiente per la pace* in which visitors could experience the tactile sensation of sand by walking barefoot on the sculpture. On this occasion he presented the film *Dunes, Water and the Venice Biennale 1976,* which shows the footprints of the artist in the sand: "I was born in the dunes on the shores of the Mediterranean. I felt for the first time beneath my bare feet the forms imprinted in the sand: soft/hard, rounded/angular, warm/cold, wet/dry. My footprints on the sand were my first sculptures, the first reliefs I ever made; the sun discovered them."

AMNON BARZEL, *Dani Karavan: Due ambienti per la pace,* Prato, Florence, 1978.

In 1971 Christo and Jeanne-Claude, in Boston, presented the project *Wrapped Walk Way*. They managed to realize it in 1978, wrapping the walkways of Loose Memorial Park in Kansas City, Missouri.

sense of space. The landscape then begins to look more like a map in three dimensions than a rustic garden."[24]

The action of *revealing new landscapes* is another consequence of the story of Tony Smith.

Smith's "dark pavement" had been extended as an object (Carl Andre) and as the absence of the object (Richard Long). Smithson, instead, puts the accent on *where* the dark road passes, on the *quality* of the landscape crossed.

The sensation of the infinite and of the end of art felt by Smith didn't only come from the dark silhouette crossing the landscape, but also from the type of landscape around it, an actual territory that had still not been investigated by art. Smithson understood that with 'earth art' new spaces were opened up for physical and conceptual experimentation, and that artists could modify the way the observer saw these territories, representing them in a new light, revealing aesthetic values: the new aesthetic discipline of *Site Selection Study* had just begun.[25] In December 1967 another article by Robert Smithson appeared in *Artforum* with the title "The Monuments of Passaic," and at the same time an exhibition of his work was inaugurated in New York at the gallery of Virginia Dwan.[26] The show included a *Negative Map Showing Region of Monuments along the Passaic River,* and twenty-four black-and-white photographs showing the monuments of Passaic. But the show was not a photo show, and the monuments are actually strange objects in the industrial landscape of the periphery. The invitation, on the other hand, was clear: the audience should rent a car and go with the artist/revealer/ guide along the Passaic River to explore a "land that time forgot."[27]

The article in *Artforum* provides some clues, and the account of the experience of the discovery of this land, a sort of parody of the diaries of travelers in the 19th century in which Smithson sets off to explore the uncharted, virgin territories of the outskirts of Passaic, his native city. Smithson defines the journey as a *suburban odyssey,* a pseudo-touristic epic that celebrates as monuments the live presences of a space in dissolution, a place that thirty years later we would have called a *non-place.* In an entirely different sense, Smithson applied the term *non-site* to the materials he extracted from the sites, which took on a negative sign once they had been decontextualized in galleries.[28]

Walkscapes – walking as an aesthetic practice

On the morning of 30 September 1967 he left his house to set off on the *Tour*. Before taking a bus to Passaic he bought a paperback novel by Brian W. Aldiss entitled *Earthworks*. As he browsed through the book he noticed, through the window, that the bus had already passed a monument, so he decided to get off the bus and continue the trip to the city on foot. The first monument was a bridge. Smithson tried to take a photograph, but the light was strange, it was like taking a photograph of a photograph. This is the moment in which reality begins to be mixed with its representation. He walks down to the banks of the river and finds an unguarded worksite, listens to the sound of a large conduit that sucks up river sludge, and then sees an artificial crater full of clear, pale water with large tubes emerging. He continues to perceive a sense of continuous disintegration. The territory appears in its primitive state, a "panorama zero," simultaneously in flight toward a future of self-destruction. Leaving the worksite he finds himself in a new territory, a used-car lot that divides the city in two: a mirror in which he cannot comprehend which side he is on. The reality of the city starts to infinitely lose itself in its dual reflection, in two representations of itself.

At the Dwan Gallery no artwork is shown, at least in the sense of an object constructed and displayed by the artist. Neither does the work exist in the place indicated on the map: the map doesn't indicate the action of the journey, and anyone who visits the site will not find a landscape altered by the artist, but the landscape just as it is, in its 'natural' state. So does the work consist in having made the journey? Or in having brought other people to the banks of the Passaic River? Is the work in the photos shown at the gallery or in those taken by the visitors? The answer is that the work is all these things combined. A series of elements (the place, the journey, the invitation, the article, the photos, the map, the earlier and subsequent writings) combine to constitute its meaning and, as in all of Smithson's works, the work itself. Even in the case of his large earthworks, once the transformation of the earth has been completed, giving rise to a work, the work is subjected to a series of extensions in all directions. Smithson continues to rework the photographic and video materials, the descriptions, always postponing a completed sense, eluding any type of definition. Smithson's works are never concluded, they remain eternally open-ended, reaching for infinity.

Before the odyssey along the Passaic River Smithson had experimented with the forms of Abstract Expressionism and Minimalist sculpture. In 1966 and 1967 he began to develop the "earthworks" for which he will be remembered in the history of art. The *Tour* took place in a moment of passage and would continue to be present in all the subsequent works. For Smithson the trips are an instinctive need for research and experience of the reality of the space around him. Journeys with the mind in hypothetical lost continents, journeys inside maps he folds, cuts and superimposes in infinite three-dimensional compositions, and journeys made with Nancy Holt and other artists to the great American deserts, to urban dumps, to abandoned quarries, to territories transformed by industry. "Toward 1965, somewhat by chance, Smithson began a series of more methodical explorations of New Jersey. [...] The preliminary phase," Nancy Holt recalls

> consisted in in-depth explorations of abandoned places overgrown by weeds, ruined houses where the staircases wound through a sort of American jungle [...] opening a path through the underbrush, groping one's way across the cracks of abandoned quarries, exploring landscapes destroyed by the actions of man. The excursion had become the focal point of Smithson's thought: they led him to gradually abandon the almost minimalist sculptures [...] and they showed him the way that was to allow his art to free itself of the social and material obligations imposed by museums and galleries.[29]

For Smithson urban exploration is the pursuit of a medium, a means to glean aesthetic and philosophical categories with which to work from the territory. One of Smithson's most extraordinary abilities lies in that constant mingling in his explorations of physical descriptions and aesthetic interpretations: the discourse crosses different planes simultaneously, loses its way on unfamiliar paths, delves into the material surrounding it, transforming the stratifications of the territory into those of the mind, as indicated in another article entitled "A Sedimentation of the Mind: Earth Projects," in which he defines his relationship with time:

Walkscapes – walking as an aesthetic practice

ROBERT SMITHSON and CARL ANDRE at the Pine Barrens, New Jersey, 1968.

"'Site Selection Study' in terms of art is just beginning. The investigation of a specific site is a matter of extracting concepts out of existing sense-data through direct perceptions. Perception is prior to conception, when it comes to site selection or definition. One does not *impose,* but rather *exposes* the site—be it interior or exterior. Interiors may be treated as exteriors or vice versa. The unknown areas of sites can best be explored by artists."

ROBERT SMITHSON, "Towards the Development of an Air Terminal Site", in *Artforum,* June 1967, republished in FLAM, JACK (ed.), *The Collected Writings, op. cit.,* p. 60.

See the Monuments of Passaic, New Jersey

"What can you find in Passaic that you cannot find in Paris, London or Rome? Find out for yourself. Discover (if you dare) the breathtaking Passaic River and the eternal monuments on its enchanted banks.

Ride in Rent-a-Car comfort to the land that time forgot. Only minutes from N.Y.C. Robert Smithson will guide you through this fabled series of sites. And don't forget your camera. Special maps come with each tour. For more information visit Dwan Gallery, 29 West 57th Street. New York."

A TOUR OF THE MONUMENTS OF PASSAIC, NEW JERSEY (1967)

ROBERT SMITHSON, "The Monuments of Passaic", in *Artforum*, December 1967, reprinted with the title "A Tour of the Monuments of Passaic", in *The Writings of Robert Smithson*, ed. NANCY HOLT, New York University Press, 1979, and Robert Smithson, *The Collected Writings*, ed. JACK FLAM, University of California Press, 1996. See also MAGGIE GILCHRIST & MARIE-SOPHIE BOULAN, *Robert Smithson, Le Paysage entropique 1960-1973*, Avignon, 1994; JEAN PIERRE CRIQUI, "Ruines à l'envers: introduction à la visite des monuments de Passaic par Robert Smithson", in *Cahiers d'Art*, Musée National d'Art Moderne, 43, Paris, 1993.

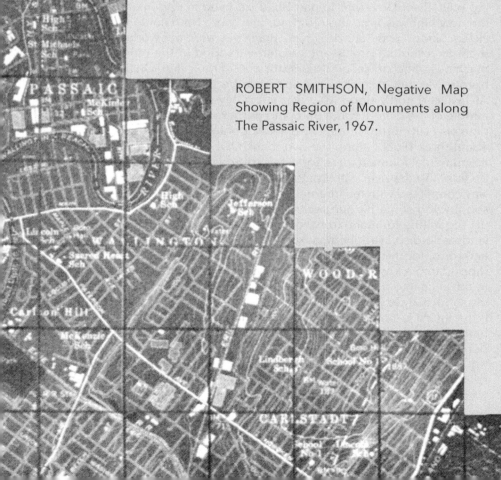

ROBERT SMITHSON, Negative Map Showing Region of Monuments along The Passaic River, 1967.

ROBERT SMITHSON, *A Tour of the Monuments of Passaic, New Jersey* (1967).

"When I walked on the bridge, it was as though I was walking on an enormous photograph that was made of wood and steel, and underneath the river existed as an enormous movie film that showed nothing but a continuous blank. [...] Along the Passaic River banks were many minor monuments such as concrete abutments that supported the shoulders of a new highway in the process of being built. River Drive was in part bulldozed and in part intact. It was hard to tell the new highway from the old road; they were both confounded into a unitary chaos. Since it was Saturday, many machines were not working, and this caused them to resemble prehistoric creatures trapped in the mud, or, better, extinct machines—mechanical dinosaurs stripped of their skin. On the edge of this pre-historic Machine Age were pre-and post-World War II suburban houses. [...] As I walked north along what was left of River Drive, I saw a monument in the middle of the river—it was a pumping derrick with a long pipe attached to it. The pipe was supported in part by a set of pontoons, while the rest of it extended about three blocks along the river bank till it disappeared into the earth. [...] a monumental fountain that suggested six horizontal smokestacks that seemed to be flooding the river with liquid smoke. The great pipe was in some enigmatic way connected with the infernal fountain. It was as though the pipe was secretly sodomizing some hidden technological orifice, and causing a monstrous sexual organ (the fountain) to have an orgasm. A psychoanalyst might say that the landscape displayed 'homosexual tendencies', but I will not draw such a crass anthropomorphic conclusion. I will merely say, 'It was there.' [...] Perhaps I had slipped into a lower stage of futurity—did I leave the real future behind in order to advance into a false future? Yes, I did. Reality was behind me at that point in my suburban Odyssey. [...]
If the future is 'out of date' and 'old fashioned', then I had been in the future. I had been on a planet that had a map of Passaic drawn over it, and a rather imperfect map at that. A sidereal map marked up with 'lines' the size of streets, and 'squares' and 'blocks' the size of buildings. At any moment my feet were apt to fall through the cardboard ground. I am convinced that the future is lost somewhere in the dumps of the non-historical past; it is in yesterday's newspapers,

n the *jejune* advertisements of science-fiction movies, in the false mirror of our rejected dreams. Time turns metaphors into *things*, and stacks them up in cold rooms, or places them in the celestial playgrounds of the suburbs. […] That zero panorama seemed to contain *ruins in reverse*, that is—all the new construction that would eventually be built. This is the opposite of the 'romantic ruin' because the buildings don't *fall* into ruin *after* they are built but rather *rise* into ruin before they are built. […]

This anti-romantic *mise-en-scène* suggests the discredited idea of *time* and many other 'out-of-date' things. But the suburbs exist without a rational past and without the 'big events' of history. Oh, maybe there are a few statues, a legend, and a couple of curios, but no past, just what passes for a future. A Utopia minus a bottom. […] Passaic seems full of 'holes' compared to New York City, which seems tightly packed and solid, and those holes in a sense are the monumental vacancies that define, without trying, the memory-traces of an abandoned set of futures. Such futures are found in grade B Utopian films, and then imitated by the suburbanite. […]

'The last monument was a sand box or a model desert. […] It suggested the sullen dissolution of entire continents, the drying up of oceans, no longer were there green forests and high mountains, all that existed were millions of grains of sand, a vast deposit of bones and stones pulverized into dust. Every grain of sand was a dead metaphor […] an open grave—a grave that children cheerfully play in. […] I should now like to prove the irreversibility of eternity by using a *jejune* experiment for proving entropy. Picture in your mind's eye the sand box divided in half with black sand on one side and white sand on the other. We take a child and have him run hundreds of times clockwise in the box until the sand gets mixed and begins to turn grey; after that we have him run anti-clockwise; but the result will not be a restoration of the original division but a greater degree of greyness and an increase of entropy. Of course, if we filmed such an experiment we would prove the reversibility of eternity by showing the film backwards, but then sooner or later the film itself would crumble or get lost and enter the state of irreversibility."

Many people would simply like to forget time, because it contains a 'principle of death' (as all artists know). Floating on this *temporal shoreline* we find the remains of the history of art, but the 'present' can no longer defend the cultures of Europe, nor the primitive or archaic civilizations; we must instead explore the pre- and post-historic spirit; we need to go where distant futures meet distant pasts.[30]

The deeper sense of the outing in Passaic is the pursuit of a "land that time forgot," in which present, past and future do not dwell, but instead different, suspended timeframes, outside of history, between science fiction and the dawn of man, fragments of time positioned in the 'actuality' of suburbia. Unlike Long, who calls him an "urban cowboy,"[31] and unlike Fulton, who admits he doesn't know how to walk in urban space,[32] Smithson delves into the refuse of the world's suburbia in pursuit of a new nature, a territory free of representation, spaces, and times in continuous transformation. The urban periphery is the metaphor for the periphery of the mind, the rejects of thought and culture. It is in these places, rather than the false archaic nature of the deserts, that it is possible to formulate new questions and hypothesize new answers. Smithson doesn't avoid the contradictions of the contemporary city, he walks straight into their midst, in an existential condition halfway between the Paleolithic hunter and the archaeologist of abandoned futures.

The Entropic Landscape

In *Entropy and the New Monuments,* written one year before the trip to Passaic, Smithson stated that certain minimal objects celebrate what Flavin called an "inactive history" and what physicists call "entropy" or "energy dispersion", the measure of energy utilized when one state is transformed into another. They were objects that confirmed the phrase of Vladimir Nabokov, for whom "the future is simply inverted obsolescence." According to Smithson, "the new monuments, rather than reminding us of the past, seem to want to make us forget the future."[33] In the empty spaces, forgotten by their very inhabitants, he recognizes the most natural *territory of forgetting,* a landscape that has taken on the character of a new entropic nature. In the *Tour* the description of the territory doesn't lead to ecological-environmental considerations regarding the destruction of the river or the industrial wastes that make the water putrid, there is a delicate balance between renunciation and accusation, between renunciation and contemplation. The judgement is exclusively aesthetic, not ethical, never ecstatic. There is no enjoyment, no satisfaction, no emotional involvement in walking through the nature of suburbia. The discourse starts with an acceptance of reality as it presents itself, and continues on a plane of general reflection in which Passaic becomes the emblem of the periphery of the occidental world, the place of scrap, of the production of a new landscape made of refuse and disruption. The monuments are not *admonishments,* but natural elements that are an integral part of this new landscape, presences that live immersed in an entropic territory: they create it, transform it, and destroy it, they are monuments self-generated by the landscape, wounds man has imposed on nature, and which nature has absorbed, transforming their meaning, accepting them in a new nature, and a new aesthetic. The new landscape that appears in suburbia calls, according to Smithson, for a new discipline capable of grasping the significance of the transformation and mutation from the natural to the artificial and vice versa:

> We live in defined structures, we are surrounded by reference systems—but nature dismantles them, taking them back to an earlier state of non-integrity. Artists today are starting to notice the strongly evanescent character of this progressive disintegration of structures. Claude Lévi-Strauss has proposed the founding of a new discipline of 'entropology'. Artists and art critics should orient their efforts in this direction.[34]

James Lingwood goes back to this statement by Smithson and explains:

According to Lévi-Strauss, the more complex the organization of a society, the greater the quantity of entropy produced. The more elaborate a given structure, the more it will be marked by disintegration. Thus primitive or 'cold' societies (whose functioning, according to Lévi-Strauss, is something like that of a pendulum mechanism) produce very little entropy; while 'warm' societies (which are more like internal combustion engines) generate an enormous quantity. The United States, the most highly developed of the warm machines, therefore generate the greater part of the disorder. Immersed in his landscapes in full disintegration, Smithson becomes the artist-entropologist of his era.[35]

1967 is the year of walking: in England and the United States we find *A Line Made by Walking* and *A Tour of the Monuments of Passaic*, two journeys which in different ways were to have a strong influence on the following generation. One year after the publication of the story of Tony Smith, that ineffable experience, extraneous to the field of art, was practiced, represented and theorized by artists who saw it as the archetype of primitive art as well as the expressive possibilities of the contemporary city. The journeys of Long moved through uncontaminated nature, where time stood still in an archaic state. To use the terminology of Lévi-Strauss, Long crosses the "cold territories," reliving a Neolithic spatial situation in pursuit of the origins of art, tracing back from the erection of the menhirs to the first traces of the path. Smithson, instead, sets off to explore the "warm territories," the industrial landscapes, territories disrupted by nature or by man, abandoned zones condemned to the oblivion of the entropic landscape. A territory in which one perceives the transient character of matter, time and space, in which nature rediscovers a new 'wilderness,' a wild, hybrid, ambiguous state, anthropically altered and then escaping man's control to be reabsorbed again by nature.

Walkscapes – walking as an aesthetic practice

Notes

[1] Gilles Tiberghien, author of the first preface to this book, has dealt with the theme of walking in the history of land art in several texts: *Land Art*, Carré, Paris 1993; *Sculptures inorganiques*, in «Les Cahiers du Musée National d'Art Moderne», 39 (1992); *Le principe de l'axolotl & suppléments*, Crestet centre d'art, Strasbourg 1998; *Nature, art et paysage*, Actes Sud / École nationale supérieure du Paysage / Centre du Paysage, Paris 2001; *Hodologique*, in aa.vv., *Cheminements*, «Les Carnets du Paysage», 11, Actes-Sud/Ensp, Paris 2004, pp. 6-25. On the same theme see also: Anne Francoise Penders, *En Chemin, le Land Art*, La lettre volée, Bruxel- les 1999; Jean Marc Besse, *Quatre notes conjointes sur l'introduction de l'ho- dologie dans la pensée contemporaine*, in aa.vv., *Cheminements* pp. 26-33.

[2] Samuel Wagstaff, *Talking with Tony Smith*, in «Artforum», december 1966, republished in Gregory Battcock (editor), *Minimal Art, a Critical Anthology*, Dutton & Co., New York 1968, p. 381. Concerning the controversy on «Artforum» after the publication of the article see: Gilles Tiberghien, Land Art cit., pp. 29-40; Rosalind Krauss, *Passages in Modern Sculpture* M.I.T. Press, Cambridge (Mass.), 1981. On Tony Smith see: Lucy Lippard, *Tony Smith*, Thames and Hudson, London 1972; Jean Pierre Criqui, *Tric- trac pour Tony Smith*, in «Artstudio», 6 (1987); Jean Pierre Criqui , *Tony Smith: Dédale, architecte et sculpteur*, in «L'Architecture d'Aujourd'hui», 286 (1993).

[3] The reference is to «When attitudes becames form», the title of the fampus exhibition cured by Harald Szeemann at the Berna's Kunsthalle in 1969.

[4] Phyllis Tuchman, *Entretien avec Carl Andre*, in *Art Minimal II*, CAPC, Bordeaux, 1987, p. 3.

[5] Claude Gintz, "Richard Long, la vision, le paysage, le temps", in *Art Press*, 104, June 1986, pp 5-7.

[6] Michael Fried, *Art and Objecthood*, «Artforum», june 1967, republished in Gregory Battcock (editor), *Minimal Art, a Critical Anthology*, Dutton & Co., New York 1968, p. 116. See also Clement Greenberg, *Modernist Painting*, in «Art Yearbook», 4 (1963), republished in Gregory Battcock (editor), *The New Art*, Dutton, New York 1966, pp. 101-2.

[7] Rosalind Krauss, *The Originality of the Avant-Garde and Other Modernist Myths*, MIT Press, Cambrigde (Mas.), 1985, trad. fr. *L'originalité de l'avant-garde et autres mythes modernistes*, Macula, Paris 1993, pp. 111-28.

[8] Ibid.

[9] Ibid.

[10] This and the other quotes came from Gilles A. Tiberghien, *Sculptures inorganiques...*, op cit., pp. 98-115, the refernces to Hegel esthetic came form the translation of Jacques Derrida, *Hegel et la pensée moderne*, Puf, Paris 1970.

[11] About the relationship between land art and neolithic art see: Lucy Lippard, *Overlay, Contemporary Art and the Art of Prehistory*, Pantheon Books, New York 1983; Kirk Varnedoe, *Contemporary explorations*, in William Rubin (a cura di), *Primitivism*

in 20th Century Art, Moma, New York 1985; Kenneth White, *L'art de la terre*, in «Ligeia», 11-12 (1992).

[12] Rudy H. Fuchs, *Richard Long*, Thames & Hudson, London/ Solomon Guggenheim Foundation, New York, 1986.

[13] Guy Tosatto, *Richard Long: Sur la route*, Musée départemental de Rochechouart, Rochechouart, 1990. About Richard Long see Jean Marc Poinsot, *Richard Long. Construire le Paysage*, «Art Presse», november 1981; Marco Meneguzzo, *Il luogo buono: Richard Long*, Pac, Milano 1985; Richard Long, *Piedras*, Ministerio de Cultura, Madrid 1986; Anne Seymour, *Richard Long, Walking in Circles*, Braziller, New York 1991, Marco Codognato, *Richard Long*, Electa, Milano 1994.

[14] Hamish Fulton, "Old Muddy", in Anne Seymour, *Richard Long: Walking in Circles*, New York 1991.

[15] About the different ways of walking of Richard Long and Hamish Fulton see Kennet White, *L'Art de la terre…*, op cit, pp 11-12.

[16] Ibid.

[17] Ibid.

[18] Claude Gintz, *Richard Long, la vision, le paysage, le temps*, in Art Press 104, June 1986, pp 5-7.

[19] The relationship between the works of Long and the great figures engraved in the English mountains is explicit in the work *A Six Day Walk over All Roads, Lanes and Double Tracks inside an Aix-Miles-Wide Circle Centered on The Giant of Cerne Abbas*, 1975. In this work the title explains the procedure. Here Long reactivates an age-old tradition of utilization of the earth as a huge canvas, a surface on which to draw messages aimed at beings from another world. The Cerne Abbas Giant is one of the large figures engraved on the terrain in England, which together with the White Horse of Uffington and the Long Man of Willington, still constitute one of the major mysteries of English culture. See also Tiberghien, *Land Art…* op. cit., p. 102.

[20] "Walks are like clouds, they came and go" is one of the best known sentences of Hamish Fulton, see Peter Turner, *An Interview with Hamish Fulton*, in Robert Adams, *Landscape Theory*, Lustrum Press, New York 1980; *An interview with Hamish Fulton*, in Common Ground: Five artists in the Florida Landscape, Sarasota Ringling Museum of Art, 1982; Hamish Fulton, *Camp Fire*, Stedelijk Van Abbemuseum, Eindoven 1985; Hamish Fulton, *One Hundred Walks*, Haags Gemente- museum, Den Haag 1991; Hamish Fulton, *Walking beside the River Vechte*, Städti- sche Galerie Nordhorn, Nordhorn 1998.

[21] On the relationship between art and cartography see the famous exhibition *Cartes et figures de la Terre*, Centre Georges Pompidou / Cci, Paris 1980. The text of Italo Calvino was a rewiew of this exibition and it has been published as *Il viandante nella mappa*, in Italo Calvino, *Collezione di sabbia*, Garzanti, Milano 1984, pp. 23- 24. See also Omar Calabrese, Roberto Giovannoli, and Isabella Pezzini (editors), *Hic sunt leones. Geografia fantastica e viaggi straordinari*, Electa, Milano 1983; Michelle Ange Brayer, *Mesures d'une fiction picturale: la carte de gèographie* , in «Exposé», 2 (1995); Michelle Ange Brayer (editor), *Cartographiques*, actes du colloqueà l'Académie de

France (Roma, 19-20 maggio 1995), Rnm, Paris 1996; Jean Marc Besse, *Voir la Terre. Six essais sur le paysage et la géographie*, Actes Sud, Arles 2000; Jean Marc Besse, *Face au monde. Atlas, jardins, géoramas*, Desclée de Brouwer, Paris 2003.

[22] Robert Smithson, "Letter to the Editor", in *Artforum*, October 1967. Reprinted in *The Writings of Robert Smithson*, ed. Nancy Holt, New York University Press, 1979, and in *Robert Smithson, The Collected Writings*, ed. Jack Flam, University of California Press, 1996, pp. 66-67.

[23] Robert Smithson, *Towards the development of an air terminal site*, in «Artforum», june 1967, republished in Robert Smithson, The Collected Writings…, op. cit., p. 60. This is the article about the project he was leading as an associate artist in the Tippets-Abbett-McCarthy-Stratton architecture studio for Dallas-Forth Worth Airport.

[24] Robert Smithson, *Aerial Art*, in «Studio International», February-april 1969, republished in *The Collected Writings…*, op. cit. p. 116.

[25] Robert Smithson, *Towards…* op. cit., p. 60.

[26] Robert Smithson, *The Monuments of Passaic*, in Artforum, December 1967, reprinted with the title *A Tour of the Monuments of Passaic*, in Nancy Holt (ed.), *The Collected Writings*, New York University Press, 1979, and Robert Smithson, *The Collected Writings*, ed. Jack Flam, University of California Press, 1996. See also Maggie Gilchrist & Marie-Sophie Boulan, *Robert Smithson, Le Paysage entropique 1960-1973*, Avignon, 1994; Jean Pierre Criqui, *Ruines à l'envers: introduction à la visite des monuments de Passaic par Robert Smithson*, in Cahiers d'Art, Musée National d'Art Moderne, 43, Paris, 1993, Gary Shapiro, *Earthwards. Robert Smithson and Art after Babel*, University of California Press, Berke- ley-London 1995.

[27] The text of the flyer is published with the title *See the Monuments of* Passaic, New Jersey, in Robert Smithson, *The Collected Writings…*, op. cit., p. 356.

[28] See Louise Cummins, *La dialectique site/non-site. Une utopie cartographique*, in «Parachute», 68 (1992), pp. 45-46.

[29] Kay Larson, *Les Excursions géologiques de Robert Smithson*, in Maggie Gilchrist & Marie-Sophie Boulan, *Robert Smithson, Le Paysage entropique 1960-1973*, Avignon, 1994, p. 40.

[30] Robert Smithson, *A Sedimentation of the mind: earth projects*, in «Artforum», september 1968, republished in Robert Smithson, *The Collected Writings…*, op. cit., p. 100.

[31] Ann Hindry, *La légèreté de l'être selon Richard Long*, in «Artstudio», Fall 1988, p. 130.

[32] In fact, in recent years Hamish Fulton's work in urban space has changed a lot. I have recently talked a lot with him about this theme and he told me about many choreographic experiences led in different cities, see for example Hamish Fulton, *Keep Moving*, Charta, Milan 2005.

[33] Robert Smithson, *Entropy and the New Monuments*, in «Artforum», june 1966, republished in Robert Smithson, *The Collected Writings*, op. cit., pp. 10-23.

[34] Robert Smithson, *Art through the Camera's Eye* (1971), in *The Collected Writings*, op. cit. p. 375.

[35] James Lingwood, *L'entropologue*, in *Le Paysage Entropique…*, op. cit., p. 29.

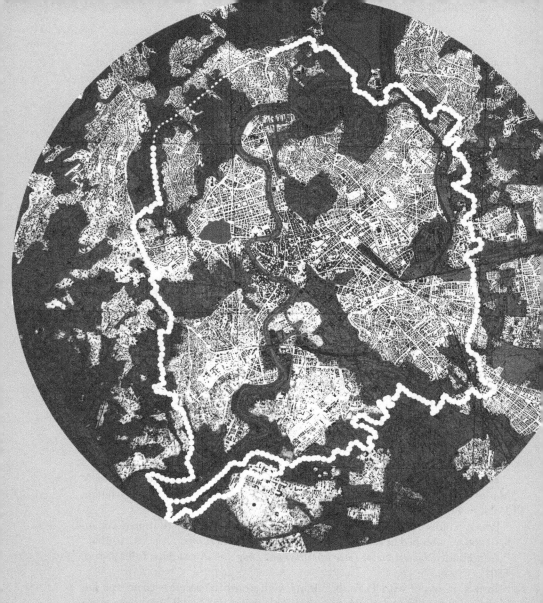

**Stalker Through the Actual Territories,
Rome, 5-8 October 1995**

Transurbance

Barefoot in the Chaos

During the same years in which Robert Smithson was exploring the empty spaces of the American peripheries, architects were trying to comprehend what was spontaneously growing in the territory before their incredulous eyes.[1] Looking up from their analyses of historical centers, typo-morphological relations, and urban tracings, architects realized that something was happening around them that they had refused to notice, and that eluded all their categories of interpretation. They couldn't understand how a sort of *cancer* had gotten hold of the city and was destroying it. Around the city something had been born that wasn't city, and which they didn't hesitate to define as 'non-city' or 'urban chaos,' a general disorder inside which it was impossible to comprehend anything except certain fragments of order randomly juxtaposed in the territory. Some of these fragments had been built by the architects themselves, others by speculators, while others still were the result of intervention originating on a regional, national or even multinational scale. The vantage point of those who observed this type of chaotic city was located inside the historical city. From this position, the architects approached the *thing* the way a doctor approaches a patient: it was necessary to *cure the cancer,* to restore order; what was happening was unacceptable, it was necessary to intervene, re-qualify, to impose *quality*. At this point it was also noticed that—once again there beside the historical city, in the 'periphery'—there were large empty spaces that were not being utilized, that could lend themselves to large-scale operations of territorial surgery. Given their large scale, they were called *urban voids*. Design would have to work on these areas and bring new portions of order into the chaos of the periphery: to reconnect and re-compose the fragments, to *saturate* and *suture* the voids with new forms of order, often extracted from the *quality* of the historical city. Even today many architects approach the cancer of the periphery with these intentions and these operative modes.

With the downfall of these positivist certainties, the debate on the contemporary city developed other categories of interpretation. Attempts were made to look at what was effectively happening and to ask why. A first step was to understand that this system of disintegration extended far beyond the limits of what had been thought of as the city, forming a true territorial system, "the diffuse city".[2] A system of low-density suburban settlement that extends outward, forming discontinuous fabric, sprawling over large territorial areas. The inhabitants of this city, the 'diffuse settlers,' were people who lived outside of the most elementary civil and urban laws, inhabiting only the private space of the home and the automobile. Their only idea of public space was the shopping mall, the highway rest stop, the gas station, and the railroad station. They would destroy any space designed for their social life. These new barbarians had invaded the city and wanted to transform it into that global Happy Valley where everyone lives in a single-family house, in a habitat whose only outward extensions are real highways and the virtual highways of the Internet.[3]

Observing this new territory that had sprouted up everywhere, in various local versions, it became increasingly evident that, apart from the new objects of anonymous building development, there was also a presence that, after having long been a mere backdrop, was increasingly the protagonist of the urban landscape. This presence was the *void*, empty or 'open' space. The model of the diffuse

Walkscapes – walking as an aesthetic practice

city effectively described what had spontaneously taken form around our cities, but once again it analyzed the territory by starting with the full parts, the solids, without observing inside the empty parts, the voids. And the inhabitants of the diffuse city, in fact, did not spend time only in houses, highways, webs, and rest stops, but also in those open spaces that had not been inserted in the system. In effect, the open spaces turned their back on the city to organize their own autonomous, parallel life, but they were inhabited. These were the places where the 'diffusion dwellers' went to grow vegetables without a permit, to walk the dog, have a picnic, make love, and look for shortcuts leading from one urban structure to another.

These were the places where their children went in search of free spaces for socializing. In other words, beyond the settlement systems, the outlines, the streets and the houses, there is an enormous quantity of empty spaces that form the background against which the city defines itself. They are different from those open spaces traditionally thought of as public spaces—squares, boulevards, gardens, parks—and they form an enormous portion of undeveloped territory that is utilized and experienced in an infinite number of ways, and in some cases turns out to be absolutely impenetrable. The voids are a fundamental part of the urban system, spaces that inhabit the city in a nomadic way, moving on every time the powers that be try to impose a new order. They are realities that have grown up outside and against the project of modernity, which is still incapable of recognizing their value and, therefore, of entering them.

The Fractal Archipelago

Observing the aerial photo of any city that has developed beyond its walls, the image that immediately springs to mind is that of an organic fabric, of a thread-like form that accumulates in more or less dense lumps. At the center the material is relatively compact, but toward the edges it expels islands detached from the rest of the constructed fabric. As the islands grow they are transformed into centers in their own right, often equivalent to the original center, forming a larger polycentric system. The result is an 'archipelago' pattern: a grouping of islands that float in a great empty sea in which the waters form a continuous fluid that penetrates the solids, branching out on various scales, all the way to the smallest abandoned nooks and crannies between the portions of constructed city. Not only are there large portions of empty territory, they are also linked by many voids on different scales and of different types that combine to constitute a ramified system that permits interconnection of the large areas that have been defined as 'urban voids.'

In spite of its apparently formless figure, the design of the city obtained by separating the full parts from the empty parts can, instead, be interpreted as a 'form' of complex geometries, or those used to describe systems that define their own structure and appear as accumulations of matter "without form."[4] If we accept the fact that the city develops in keeping with a natural dynamic similar to that of the clouds or the galaxies, it follows that this process will be difficult to program and predict, due to the quantity of forces and variables involved. But observing the process of growth, we can see that the islands, as they expand, leave empty areas inside themselves, and form figures with irregular borders that have the characteristic of "autosimilarity", an intrinsic property of fractal structures: on the different scales we can observe the same phenomena, like the irregular distribution of full zones, the continuity of empty areas and the irregular borders that permit the void to penetrate the solids. This system, by nature, does not simply tend to saturate itself, filling the spaces that have remained empty; it also tends to expand, leaving a system of voids in its interior. While the original center has less *probability* of developing and changes more slowly, at the edges of the system the transformations are more probable and rapid. At the margins we find those landscapes Lévi-Strauss would define as *warm* and Robert Smithson would define as *entropic*. Urban space-time has different speeds: from the stasis of the centers to the continuous transformation of the margins. At the center time stands still, transformations are frozen, and when they happen they are so evident that they cannot conceal any-thing unexpected: they happen under the close surveillance and rigid control of the city. At the margins, on

Walkscapes – walking as an aesthetic practice

the other hand, we find a certain dynamism and we can observe the coming-into-being of a vital organism that transforms itself, leaving entire parts of the territory in a state of abandon around and inside itself, in a situation that is difficult to control.

It is important to emphasize the self-representative character of the fractal archipelago form: our civilization has constructed it on its own to define its own image, in spite of the theories of architects and town planners. The empty spaces that define its figure are the places that best represent our civilization in its unconscious, multiple becoming. These *urban amnesias* are not only waiting to be *filled with things,* they are living spaces to be filled with meanings. Therefore we are not looking at a non-city to be transformed into city, but at a parallel city with its own dynamics and structures that have yet to be fully understood.[5]

As we have seen, the city can be described from an aesthetic-geometric, but also an aesthetic-experiential, point of view. To recognize a geography within the supposed chaos of the peripheries, therefore, we can attempt to establish a relationship with it by utilizing the aesthetic form of the erratic journey. What we discover is a complex system of public spaces that can be crossed without any need for borders or buffers. The voids of the archipelago represent the last place where it is possible to get lost within the city, the last place where we can feel we are beyond surveillance and control, in dilated, extraneous spaces, a spontaneous park that is neither the environmentalist's re-creation of a false rustic nature nor the consumer-oriented exploitation of free time. The voids are a public space with a nomadic character, that lives and is transformed so rapidly that it eludes the planning schedules of any administration.

If we climb over a wall and set off on foot in these zones we find ourselves immersed in that amniotic fluid that supplied the life force of that unconscious of the city described by the Surrealists. The liquid image of the archipelago permits us to see the immensity of the open sea, but also what is submerged there, on the seabed, at different depths, or just below the surface. Plunging into the system of voids and starting to explore its capillary inlets, we can see that what we have been accustomed to calling 'empty' isn't really so empty after all; instead, it contains a range of different identities. The sea is formed by different seas, by a congeries of heterogeneous territories positioned beside one another. These seas, if approached with a certain predisposition for crossing borders and penetrating zones, turn out to be utterly navigable, so much so that often by following the paths already traced by the inhabitants, we can walk all around the city without ever actually entering it. The city turns out to be a space of *staying* entirely crisscrossed by the territories of *going*.

Zonzo

In Italian *andare a Zonzo* means "to waste time wandering aimlessly."[6] It's an idiomatic expression whose origins have been forgotten, but it fits perfectly into the context of the city wandered by the *flâneurs,* and the streets roamed by the artists of the avant-gardes of the 1920s, or the sites of the 'driftings' of the youthful Lettrists after World War II. Today Zonzo has been profoundly changed, a new city has grown up around it, formed of different cities, crossed by the seas of the void. When "going to Zonzo" at the beginning of the last century, one was always aware whether the direction of the wanderings led toward the center or toward the outskirts. If we imagine walking through the Zonzo of yesteryear in a straight line from the center to the outskirts, first we encounter the denser zones of the center, then rarefied zones of small buildings and villas, followed by the suburbs, the industrial zones and, finally, the countryside. At this point we could have found a lookout point, to enjoy the view: a unitary, reassuring image of the city surrounded by countryside.

Following the same route today, the sequence of spaces is no longer so simple. We encounter a series of interruptions and reprises, fragments of constructed city and unbuilt zones that alternate in a continuous passage from full to empty and back. What we thought of as a compact city is actually full of holes, often inhabited by different ethnic groups. If we get lost, we cannot easily figure out how to head toward an *outside* or an *inside*. And if we do manage to find a high spot from which to observe the panorama, the view will no longer be very reassuring: it would be hard to recognize, in this strange magma,

Walkscapes – walking as an aesthetic practice

a city with a center and a periphery. Instead we are faced with a sort of leopard-skin with empty spots inside the constructed city and full spots in the middle of the countryside. Getting lost outside the walls of Zonzo today is a very different experience, but we believe that the modes and categories made available by the artistic experiences we have analyzed can help us to understand and transform this situation without erasing its identity.

Dada had discovered, in the tourist-attracting heart of Zonzo, the existence of a banal, quotidian city in which to continuously run into unexpected relations; with an act of attribution of aesthetic value, the 'urban readymade,' it revealed the existence of a city that opposed both the hyper-technological utopias of the Futurist city and the pseudo-cultural city of tourism. The Dadaists understood that the entertainment system of the tourist industry had transformed the city into a simulation of itself, and therefore they wanted to call attention to *the nonentity*, to reveal the cultural void, to exalt banality, the absence of any meaning. The Surrealists realized that something was hidden inside the void indicated by Dada, and they understood that it could be filled with values. Deambulating in the banal places of Zonzo, they defined this void as the *unconscious city:* a large sea in whose amniotic fluid we can find what the city has repressed, territories never investigated but dense with continuous discoveries. Rejection and the absence of control had produced extraneous, spontaneous places inside Zonzo, that could be analyzed like the human psyche, and the Situationists, with their psychogeography, proposed a tool for their investigation. The Surrealist-Situationist city is a living, empathic organism with its own unconscious, with spaces that elude the project of modernism and live and transform themselves independently of the will of the urbanists and, often enough, of the inhabitants themselves. The *dérive* made it possible to steer one's way through this sea and to direct the point of view in a *non-random* way toward those zones that more than others appeared to embody an *elsewhere* capable of challenging the society of the spectacle. The Situationists sought out, in the bourgeois city of the postwar era, the places forgotten by the dominant culture, off the map of the tourist itineraries: working-class neighborhoods off the beaten track, places

STALKER Manifesto, 1996
(text by Lorenzo Romito)

STALKER is a collective subject that engages research and actions within the landscape with particular attention to the areas around the city's margins and forgotten urban space, and abandoned areas or regions under transformation. These investigations are conducted across several levels, around notions of practicality, representations and interventions on these spaces that are referred to here as "Actual Territories." Stalker is together custodian, guide and artist for these "Actual Territories." In the multiple roles we are disposed to confront at once the apparently unsolvable contradictions of salvaging through abandonment, of representation through sensorial perception, of intervening within the unstable and mutable conditions of these areas.

THE ACTUAL TERRITORIES constitute the built city's negative, the interstitial and the marginal, spaces abandoned or in the process of transformation. These are the removed *lieu de la memoirs*, the unconscious becoming of the urban systems, the spaces of confrontation and contamination between the organic and the inorganic, between nature and artifice. Here the metabolization of humanity's discarded scrap, or nature's detritus, produces a new horizon of unexplored territories, mutant and by default virgin, that are for Stalker "Actual Territories." The term "actual" indicates the process in which space comes into being. The "actual" is not what we are, but rather that we are becoming, that is to say the "other" that becomes other (Foucault). Such territories are difficult to render intelligible and therefore projectable, because they lack connections to the present and therefore are extraneous to contemporary language. Their conscious presence cannot come about by direct experience, they are to be physically witnessed rather than represented. The archive of experiences is the only form of mapping possible for these "Actual Territories."

ENTERING THE TERRITORIES, perceiving the discarded territories, in completing such a route, between that which is secure, quotidian, and that which is uncertain, generates a sense of dislocation, a state of apprehension. This altered state induces a perceptual intensification unexpectedly giving the space a meaning, making "everywhere" a place for discovery, or instead a dreaded place for an undesirable encounter. The gaze becomes penetrating, the ear becomes keen to every sound.

CROSSING THE TERRITORIES on foot establishes an unmediated experience, allowing for a more dynamic reading. A nomadic research, a mode of capturing the act of crossing without regimentation, ratification or definition of the object examined, so as not to prevent its becoming. Crossing is for Stalker a creative act, that means creating a system of relations within the chaotic juxtaposition of time and space that characterizes "Actual Territories." Crossing means composing in a single conscious parcours the strident contradictions that animate these spaces, in a search for unedited harmony.

Crossings and making crossings, inducing into the perception of the actual because it can become diffused into the general consciousness, while avoiding, however, banalizing its linguistic meaning.

PERCEIVING THE BECOMING, intensifying perception, making one available to listen, is a necessary condition in order that the territories unveil themselves to those who desire crossing them. Making oneself available to perceive the unconscious language of mutation, opens an interrogation within the given pretense of describing and identifying. It stimulates an actual transcendence, in that of an inexhaustible perception of existing signifiers through continuous movement. It is the event that escapes without disappearing (Tiziana Villani) It is the objective in perceiving the scraps of atemporal spaces in a time continuum.

It is the objective of signaling our contact's trace with that object and spectacle, in as much as it vibrates our gaze, our touch, our ears, our sense of risk, our sense of destiny. It is no longer about providing information but about depositing testimony. (Merleau Ponty).

FRACTAL ORGANIZATION. Stalker, confronted by the study of complex geometries, considers that the amount of marginal area in relation to an organism's surface is an index of its wealth, given that it is as much the articulation of voids, at diverse scales, that determines the very structure of an organism. The voids constitute that "background" on which to read the form of the city that would otherwise appear homogeneous, deprived of a complex evolutionary dynamic and therefore of life itself.

CONTINUITY AND PENETRATION OF "ACTUAL TERRITORIES" THROUGH THE CITY. To defend the "Actual Territories," to guarantee the maximum of continuity and of penetration within systems of urbanization, is to enrich and give life to the city through the continuous and diffused confrontation with the unknown. In this way it will be possible to recover within the profound heart of the city, the wild, the non-planned, the nomadic.

THE ABANDONMENT. The attempt at defining and controlling the entire territory, mirage of our western culture, just when it seemed most likely to realize itself, gives forth its first water. The first cracks have opened in the very hearts of our system: the large cities. The forest that at one time surrounded cities and villages, where bears and wolves, but also the nightmares would hide, where the fantasies and the very idea of liberty itself were shoved far from the city, put into the corners, restricted and in an unbelievable act of clemency, protected. And here it is now that that same forest rises again, exactly there in the cities where the territory's systems of appropriation and control are most ancient and crumbling. Given the impossibility of total human control, the concrete under which the forests were covered has cracked open, the earth flowers in new and unpredictable forms, preparing to contest with its human occupants the domination of space, from the scrap-heaps and beyond. To forecast the unforecastable, to save the coming into being of the "Actual Territories," means to abandon them. For abandonment is the maximum form of a cure for that which has developed outside human will and plan.

THE PROJECT. To intervene on a territory is not merely an act of planning but an act of creation, an attempt to assemble contradictions and transform them into poetic relationships: ultimately one is more attentive to modifying how space is perceived than the way space itself exists.

Stalker Manifesto has been written by Lorenzo Romito in January 1996, during the exibition *Mappe*, at the Galleria Care off in Milan, curated by Emanuela de Cecco, and published in many languages on the website: http://digilander.libero.it/stalkerlab/tarkowsky/manifesto/manifest.htm. For a more in-depth view of Stalker work at that time see: Flaminia Gennari, *Progett/Azioni: tra i nuovi esploratori della città contemporanea*, "Flash Art" n° 200/1996, pp. 62-64; Emanuela de Cecco, *Non volendo aggiungere altre cose al mondo*, "Flash Art" n° 200/1996, p. 64; Lorenzo Romito, *Stalker*, in Peter Lang (ed.), *Suburban Discipline*, Princeton Architectural Press, New York 1997, pp. 130-141; *Stalker, A Travers les Territoires Actuels / Aattraverso i Territori Attuali*, Jean Michel Place, Paris 2000.

in which great multitudes lived, often far from the gaze of the society, waiting for a revolution that never happened. The concepts of psychogeography, the *dérive* and unitary urbanism, once combined with the values of the nomadic universe, had produced the city in permanent transit of Constant, a city aimed at being just the opposite of the sedentary nature of Zonzo.

New Babylon was a system of enormous empty corridors extending across the territory, permitting the continuous migration of the multicultural populations. Empty corridors for nomadic wandering took the place of the consolidated city, superimposing themselves on the land like a formless, continuous, communicating spiderweb, in which life would be an adventure. But if we venture today into the empty wrinkles of Zonzo we get the impression that New Babylon has finally been realized. The seas of Zonzo are like a New Babylon without any mega-structural or hyper-technological aspects. They are empty spaces like deserts, but like deserts they are not so empty after all; in fact, they are city. Empty corridors that penetrate the consolidated city, appearing with the extraneous character of a nomadic city living inside the sedentary city.

New Babylon lives inside the amnesias of the contemporary city like an enormous desert system ready to be inhabited by nomadic transurbance. It is a sequence of connected sectors, no longer elevated above the ground, but immersed in the city itself. Inside the wrinkles of Zonzo, spaces in transit have grown up, territories in continuous transformation in time and space, seas crossed by multitudes of 'outsiders' who hide in the city. Here new forms of behavior appear, new ways of dwelling, new spaces of freedom. The nomadic city lives in osmosis with the settled city, feeding on its refuse and offering, in exchange, its presence as a new nature, a forgotten future spontaneously produced by the entropy of the city. New Babylon has emigrated, it has left the outskirts of Passaic, crossed the oceans and reached culturally different, ancient climes, raising interesting issues of identity. Venturing into New Babylon can be a useful method for the interpretation and transformation of those zones of Zonzo that, in recent years, have thrown the disciplines of architecture and urban planning into crisis. And thanks to the artists who have roamed

Walkscapes – walking as an aesthetic practice

its interior, this city is visible today and appears as one of the most important unresolved problems of architectural culture. To design a nomadic city would seem to be a contradiction in terms. Perhaps it must be done in keeping with the manner of the Neo-Babylonians: transforming it playfully from the inside out, modifying it during the journey, restoring life to the primitive aptitude for the play of relations that permitted Abel to dwell in the world.

Good transurbance.

Notes

[1] The references are to the two fundamental texts: Kevin Linch, *The Image of the City*, University Press, Cambridge 1960; Robert Venturi, Denise Scott Brown and Steven Izenour, *Learning from Las Vegas*, M.I.T. press, 1972.

[2] On the Italian sprawl, that is called *città diffusa*, see: Bernardo Secchi, *Analisi delle strutture territoriali*, Franco Angeli, Milano 1965; Stefano Boeri, Bernardo Secchi e Livia Piperno, *I territori abbandonati*, Compositori, Bologna 1990; AA.VV., *La città diffusa*, Daest, Università di Venezia, 1990; Bernardo Secchi, *La periferia*, in «Casabella», 583 (1991); Jean Francois Lyotard, *Periferie*, in «Millepiani», 2 (1994); AA.VV., *Itaten. Indagine sulle trasformazioni del territorio italiano*, Bari 1996; Gabriele Basilico e Stefano Boeri, *Sezioni del paesaggio italiano*, Art&, Udine 1997, p. 13; Stefano Boeri, Arturo Lanzani and Edoardo Marini, *Il territorio che cambia*, Editrice Abitare Segesta, Milano 1993; Stefano Boeri, *I detective dello spazio*, in «Il Sole 24 Ore», 16 marzo 1997; Stefano Boeri, *Eclectic Atlases*, in «Documenta 3», Kassel 1997.

[3] About the themes of non-site, urban heterotopics and the poetics of terrain vagues see: Marc Augé, *Non-lieux. Introduction à une anthropologie de la surmodernité*, Seuil, Paris 1992; MIchel Foucault, *Eterotropia, luoghi e non-luoghi metropolitani*, in «Millepiani», 2 (1994); Paolo Desideri, *La città di latta*, Costa & Nolan, Genova 1995; AA.VV., *Architettura della sparizione, architettura totale*, in «Millepiani», 7 (1995); Massimo Ilardi, *L'individuo in rivolta. Una riflessione sulla miseria della cittadinanza*, Costa & Nolan, Genova 1995; Massimo Ilardi, *La città senza luoghi*, Costa & Nolan, Genova 1995; Ignasi de Solá Morales, *Urbanité Intersticielle*, in «Inter Art Actuel», 61 (1995), p. 27; Ignasi de Solá Morales, *Terrain Vague*, in «Quaderns», 212 (1996); Ignasi de Solá Morales, *Città tagliate. Appunti su identità e differenze*, in: *I racconti dell'abitare*, Editrice Abitare Segesta, Milano 1996; *L'architetto come sismografo*, Biennale di Architettura di Venezia, Milano 1996; Mirko Zardini (ed.), *Paesaggi ibridi*, Skira, Milano 1996; Paolo Desideri e Massimo Ilardi (editors), *Attraversamenti*, Costa & Nolan, Genova 1997.

Walkscapes – walking as an aesthetic practice

⁴ The concepts here are the contribution of astrophysicist Francesco Sylos Labini to the Stalker urban art laboratory. His research on the application of fractal geometry to the description of the distribution of galaxies in the universe gave the lab a fundamental contribution to understanding the urban dynamics of the fractal archipelago. See also Michael Batty and Paul Longley, *Fractal Cities: a Geometry of Form and Function*, Academic, San Diego 1994; Pierre Frankhauser, *La fractalité des structures urbaines*, Anthropos, Paris 1994; Michael Batty, *New ways of looking at cities*; Francesco Careri, *Rome archipel fractal, voyage dans les combles de la ville*, in «Techniques & Architecture», 427 (1996).

⁵ The following reflections came from the research carried out in the Stalker urban art laboratory at the beginning of the 90's. The name Stalker is a tribute to 1979's Andrej Tarkovskij's homonymous movie, which takes place in the mutant zone, a land where nature, after landing extraterrestrials, has developed its own autonomous evolution. The *zone* is blocked and fenced and the Stalker are the *passeurs*, the guides who know the gates and the access modes, who have a strategy of walking. "Stalker through the Actual Territories" is the title of the first suburban drift conducted in Rome by the lab in October 1995. Adapting the concept of the "unconscious territory" of the surrealists and the "objective passionate terrain" of the situationnists, Stalker has conducted his first erratic paths taking the concept of "actual territory" of Robert Smithson read in the key of Foucault, where the actual "is not what we are, but rather what we are becoming, that is the Other, our becoming-Other", MIchel Foucault, *Eterotropia…*, op. cit., p. 53.

⁶ Zonzo in Italian language indicates a sort of metaphorical place of wandering. It is used only in the sense "go to Zonzo", to stroll, to walk without a goal, to waste time: "Instead of studying, he goes *to zonzo*". It seems that the first time that *zonzo* appears officially in the Italian language is in the translation of the famous book of Jerome K. Jerome, *Three Men on the Bummel*, London, 1900, translated into Italian in *Tre uomini a zonzo*. Probably the word *zonzo* is likely to be an onomatopoeic derivation from *zone*, from the Greek *zonninai* which means to "crawl", "to go around", a verb daily used by the Athenian peripatetics. In Paris *la zone* still indicates that band on the edge of the industrial city where fleas markets are. In this sense, *zonzo* seems to be almost a shamanic repetition dzion zon = to go to the Zone, an exotic place where to find strange objects and to have unexpected encounters. It is here, between the Périphérique extérieur and the intérieur one, that in 1927 George Lacombe turns the film *La Zone*, a territory at the edge of modernity, whose entropy is represented in the film by an uninterrupted flow of rubbish that feeds a whole derelict humanity.

Bibliography

Errare Humanum est...

AA.VV., *Errantes, nomades et voyageurs*, Centre George Pompidou, Paris 1980

AA.VV., *Strade*, edited by Anderson Stanford, Dedalo, Bari 1982

AA.VV., *Qu'est-ce qu'une route?*, «Les Cahiers de médiologie» n° 2, Paris 1997

AA.VV., *L'esthétique de la rue*, colloque d'Amiens, L'Harmattan, Paris 1998

Albrecht, Benno e Benevolo, Leonardo, *I confini del paesaggio umano*, Laterza, Bari 1994.

Albrecht, Benno e Benevolo, Leonardo, *Le origini dell'Architettura*, Laterza, Bari 2002.

Angioni, Giulio, *I pascoli erranti. Antropologia del pastore in Sardegna*, Liguori Editore, Napoli 1989

Atzeni, Enrico, *La statuaria antropomorfa sarda*, Atti del Congresso Internazionale di La Spezia e Pontremoli, La Spezia 1994

Atzeni, Enrico, *La scoperta delle Statue –Menhir. Trent'anni di ricerche archeologiche nel territorio di Laconi*, Cuec, Cagliari 2004

Atzeni, Sergio, *Passavamo sulla terra leggeri*, Il Maestrale, Nuoro 1997

Atzori, Gianni, e Sanna Gigi, *Omines. Dal neolitico all'età nuragica*, Castello, Cagliari 1996

Balbo, F., Bertoglio, R., *Pregare con i piedi*, Edizioni Ancora, 2008

Beltrami, Vanni, *Breviario per nomadi*, Voland, Roma 2010

Benevolo, Leonardo, *La cattura dell'infinito*, Laterza, Bari 1991

Breizh, Arthur, *Le ossa del drago. Sentieri magici dai menhir ai celti*, Keltia, Aosta 1996

Burckhardt, Lucius, *Promenadologie*, in "Le design au-delà du visible", Centre George Pompidou, Paris 1991

Calabrese, Omar, Giovannoli Renato, Pezzini Isabella, *Hic sunt leones, Geografia fantastica e viaggi straordinari*, Electa, Milano 1983

Cazenave, Michel, *Enciclopédie de Simboles*, La Pochothèque L.G.F., Paris 1996

Chialà, Sabino, *Parole in Cammino*, Qiqajon Comunità di Bose, Magnano 2006

Chatwin, Bruce, *The Songlines* (1987), trad. It. *Le vie dei canti*, Adelphi, Milano 1995

Chevalier, Jean et Gheerbrant, Alain, *Dictionnaire des Symboles*, Lafont/Jupiter, Paris 1969

Childe Vere, Gordon., *Preistoria della società europea*, Sansoni, Firenze 1962

Clark, Grahame e Piggott, Stuart, *Le società preistoriche*, Mondadori, Milano 1991

De Certeau, Michel, *L'invention du quotidien. Art de faire*, Gallimard, Paris 1990

De Landa, Manuel (1997), *Mille anni di storia non lineare. Rocce, germi e parole*, instar libri, Torino 2003

Deleuze, Gilles e Guattari, Felix, *Nomadologia*, Castelvecchi, Roma 1995

Demetrio, Duccio, *Filosofia del camminare. Esercizi di meditazione mediterranea*, Cortina Raffaello 2005

Diamond, Jared, *Armi, acciaio e malattie. Breve storia del mondo negli ultimi tredicimila anni*, Einaudi, Torino 1998

Esiodo, *Teogonia*, Oscar Mondadori, Milano 2004

Feo, Giovanni, *Geografia sacra. Il culto della madre terra dalla preistoria agli etruschi*, stampa alternativa, Viterbo 2006

Feo, Giovanni, *Prima degli etruschi. I miti della grande dea e dei giganti alle origini della civiltà in Italia*, stampa alternativa, Viterbo 2001

Frau,Sergio, *Le colonne d'Ercole. Un' inchiesta*, neon, Roma 2002

Frazer, James G. (1910), *Il ramo d'oro. Studio sulla magia e la religione*, Newton Compton, Roma 1992

Giedion, Sigfried, *The Eternal Present* (1964), trad. It. *L'eterno presente*, Feltrinelli, Milano 1965

Giedion, Sigfried, *La concezione dello spazio nella preistoria*, "Casabella" n° 206, 1956

Gimbutas, Marija (1989), Il linguaggio della Dea. Mito e culto della Dea Madre nell'Europa Neolitica, Longanesi, Milano 1990

Gimbutas, Marija (1999), *Le dee viventi*, Medusa, Milano 2005

Girard, Christian, *Architecture et concepts nomades; traité d'indiscipline*, Pierre Mardaga, Bruxelles 1986

Glowczewski, Barbara, *YAPA. Peintres aborigènes*, Baudoin Lebon, Paris 1991

Guilane, Jean, *La preistoria da un continente all'altro*, Gremese, Roma 1995

Haizer, Robert Fleming, *L'età dei giganti*, Marsilio, Venezia 1990

Heidegger, Martin, *Holzwege* (1962), trad. It. *Holzwege. Sentieri erranti nella selva*, Bompiani, Milano 2002

Hesse, Hermann, *Il viandante*, Milano, Oscar Mondadori, 1993.

Janni, Paolo, *La mappa e il periplo. Cartografia antica e spazio odologico*, Università di Macerata, Giorgio Bretschneider, Roma 1984

Jullien, Francois, *éloge de la fadeur*, Editions Philippe Picquier, Paris 1991

Jesi, Fulvio, *Il linguaggio delle pietre*, Rizzoli, Milano 1978

La Cecla, Franco, *Perdersi, l'uomo senza ambiente*, Laterza, Bari 1988

La Cecla, Franco, *Mente locale. Per un'antropologia dell'abitare*, elèuthera, Milano 1993

Lanzmann, Jaques, *L' arte di camminare*, Torino, EDT, 1990

Laureano, Pietro, *Giardini di pietra. I sassi di Matera e la civiltà mediterranea*, Bollati Boringhieri, Torino 1993

Le Breton, David, *Il mondo a piedi : elogio della marcia*, Milano, Feltrinelli, 2001

Leed, Eric J., *La mente del viaggiatore. Dall'Odissea al turismo globale*, Il mulino, Bologna 1992

Leria, Michael M, *Street Zen : l'arte di camminare in meditazione*, RED, Como1998

Leroi-Gourhan, André, *Le religioni della preistoria*, Adelphi, Milano 1993

Lilliu, Giovanni, *La civiltà dei sardi, dal paleolitico all'età dei nuraghi*, Nuova ERI, Torino 1963.

Maffessoli, Michel, *Du nomadisme, vagabondages initiatiques*, Librairie Génerale Francaise, Paris 1997

Malagrinò, Paolo, *Dolmen e menhir di Puglia*, Schena, Fasano 1982

Maxia, Carlo, *Filàdas. Caprari nel Gerrei*, Cuec, Cagliari 2005

Milani, Raffaele, *Il paesaggio è un'avventura. Invito al piacere di viaggiare e di guardare*, Feltrinelli 2005

Melis, Leonardo, *Shardana. I popoli del mare*, PTM, Mogoro 2002

Morgan, Marlo, *Mutant Message Down Under* (1991), trad. It. *…e venne chiamata Due Cuori*, Sonzongo, Milano 1994

Morris, Desmond, *The Naked Ape* (1967), trad. It. *La scimmia nuda*, Bompiani, Milano 1968

Moscati, Sabatino, *Luci sul Mediterraneo*, Quasar, Roma 1995

North, John, *Stonehenge* (1996), trad. It. *Il mistero di Stonehenge*, Piemme, Alessandria 1997

Norberg-Schulz, Christian, *Existence, Space and Architecture* (1971), trad. It. *Esistenza Spazio e Architettura*, Officina, Roma 1982

Potts, Rolf, *Vagabonding*, Ponte alle grazie, Milano 2003

Pallottini, Mariano, *Alle origini della città europea*, Quasar, Roma 1985

Rykwert, Joseph, *La strada: utilità della sua storia*, in AA. VV. "Strade", edited by Stanford Anderson, Dedalo, Bari 1982

Sansot, Pierre, *Sul buon uso della lentezza*, Net, Milano 2003

Sansot, Pierre, *Passeggiate: una nuova arte del vivere*, Pratiche, Milano 2001

Schelle, Karl Gottlob, *L'arte di andare a passeggio*, Palermo, Sellerio, 1993

Sebald, Winfried Georg (1998), *Il passeggiatore solitario. In ricordo di Robert Walser*, Adelphi Milano, 2006

Sennett, Richard, *The Conscience of the Eye* (1992), trad. It. *La coscienza dell'occhio*, Feltrinelli, Milano 1992

Sobel, Dava (1995), *Longitudine. La vera storia della scoperta avventurosa che ha cambiato l'arte della navigazione*, Rizzoli, Milano1999

Strehlow, Theodor G.H., *Central Australian Religion. Personal Monototemism in a Polytotemic Community*, Flinders Press, South Australia 1993, trad. It. *I sentieri dei sogni. La religione degli aborigeni dell'Australia centrale*, Mimesis, Milano 1997

Ribichini, Sergio, *Il riso sardonico. Storia di un proverbio antico*, Carlo Delfino, Sassari 2003

Rousseau, Jean Jacques (1770), *le fantasticherie del passeggiatore solitario*, Torino, Einaudi 1993

Testa, Italo (edited by), *Pensieri viandanti: antropologia ed estetica del camminare* 2007, Diabasis, Reggio Emilia 2008

Testa, Italo (edited by), *Pensieri viandanti. L'etica del camminare*. Vol. 2, Diabasis, Reggio Emilia 2009

Thoreau, Henry David (1851), *Walden,* (con prefazione di Wu Ming 2), Donzelli 2007

Thoreau, Henry, *Camminare* (1862), Mondadori, Milano, 1991.

Turner, Edith e Turner, Victor, *Il pellegrinaggio*, Argo, Lecce 1997

Turri, Eugenio, *Gli uomini delle tende*, Comunità, Milano 1983

Vallet, Odon, *Trois marcheurs: Bouddha, Jésus, Mahomet*, in AA.VV., *Qu'est-ce qu'une route?*, "Les Cahiers de médiologie" n° 2, Paris 1997

Vergari, Alessandro, *Il manuale del camminare lento*, Cesena, Macroedizioni, 2001

Walser, Robert (1919), *La Promenade*, Gallimard, Paris 1987

White, Kenneth, *Déambulations dans l'espace nomade*, Crestet centre d'art, Arles 1995

White, Kenneth, *L'art de la terre* , in «Ligeia» n°11-12, Paris, 1992

Wright, Frank Lloyd, *The living City,* (1958) trad. It. *La città vivente*, Einaudi, Torino 1991

Zanini, Piero, *Significati del confine*, Mondadori, Milano 1997

Zarattini, Silvio, *A piedi. Condizione necessaria per entrare nelle cose*, Edizioni Il pozzo di Giacobbe, 2004

Zavalloni, Gianfranco, *La pedagogia della lumaca*, EMI, Bologna 2008

Zonchello, Salvatore Angelo, *Il culto fallico in Sardegna e presso altri popoli della terra*, Gallizzi, Sassari, 1982

Anti-Walk

AA.VV., *Cartes et figures de la terre*, Centre George Pompidou/CCI, Paris 1980

AA.VV., *André Breton*, Centre George Pompidou/CCI, Paris 1991

AA.VV., *La Ville-The City*, "Parachute" 68, 1992

AA.VV., *Internazionale Situazionista 1958-69*, Nautilus/Stampatre, Torino 1994

AA.VV., *L'art et la ville*, Centre George Pompidou, Paris 1994

AA.VV., *L'arte Dada della negazione*, De Luca, Roma 1994

AA.VV., *Pertes d'inscription*, «Exposé» 2, Orléans 1995

AA.VV., *Les Figures de la marche*, RMN, Antibes - Lyon 2000

AA.VV., «Le visiteur» n°4 e 5, Printemps 2000

Andreotti, Libero e Costa Xavier, *Situacionistas: arte, polìtica, urbanismo,* Museu d'Art Contemporani de Barcelona, ACTAR, Barcelona 1996

Andreotti, Libero, *Play tactics of the Internationale Situationniste*, "October" 91, M.I.T. Press, Cambridge MA 2000

Aragon, Louis, *Le paysan de Paris*, Gallimard, Paris 1926

a.titolo, *Zebra Crossing*, a.titolo, Torino 1998

Balzac, Honoré de, *Théorie de la démarche* (1833), trad. it. *Teoria del camminare*, Sugarco, Varese 1993

Bandini, Mirella, *Pinot Gallizio e il Laboratorio Sperimentale d'Alba,* Galleria Civica di Arte Moderna, Torino 1974

Bandini, Mirella, *La vertigine del moderno - percorsi surrealisti*, Officina, Roma 1986

Bandini, Mirella, *L'estetico, il politico: Da Cobra all'Internazionale Situazionista 1948-1957*, Officina, Roma 1977

Banham, Reyner, *Megastructure,* London 1976 trad. It. *Le tentazioni dell'architettura. Megastrutture,* Laterza, Bari 1980

Benjamin, Walter, *Paris, Capitale du XIX siècle; le livre des passages,* trad. It. Tiedemann, Rolf e Ganni, Enrico edited by, *Opere complete di Walter Benjamin. IX. I « passages di Parigi »,* Einaudi, Torino 2000

Berenstein, Jacques Paola, *Elogio aos errantes,* edufba, Salvador do Bahia 2012

Berreby, Gerard, *Documents relatifs à la fondation de l'Internationale Situationniste 1948-1957,* Allia, Paris 1985

Berreby, Gerard., *Ralph Rumney, Le Consul,* Allia, Paris 1999

Bertolino Giorgina, Comisso Francesca e Roberto Maria Teresa, *Pinot Gallizio. Il laboratorio della scrittura,* Charta, Milano 2005

Bonito, Oliva Achille, *Le tribù dell'Arte,* Galleria Comunale d'Arte Moderna, Roma 2001

Breton, André, *Manifeste du Surréalisme* (1924), in *Manifestes du Surréalisme,* Pauvert, Paris 1962

Breton, André, *Nadja,* N.R.F., Paris 1928

Careri, Francesco, *Constant / New Babylon, una città nomade,* Testo & Immagine, Torino 2001

Careri, Francesco, Linke Armin e Vitone Luca, *Constant e le radici di New Babylon,* "Domus" n° 885, 2005

Chtcheglov, Ivan alias Gilles, Ivain, *Formulaire pour un Urbanisme Nouveau,* (1953) ripubblicato in "I.S." n°1, p.15

Constant, *New Babylon,* Haags Gemeentemuseum, Den Haag 1974

Debord, Guy E., *Introduction a une critique de la géographie urbaine,* «Les Lèvres Nues» n° 6, pp. 11-15, Bruxelles, settembre 1955.

Debord, Guy E., *Théorie de la dérive,* «Les Lèvres Nues» n° 8/9, 1956 ripubblicato nel 1958 in «I. S.» n° 2, p. 20.

Debord, Guy E., *La société du spectacle,* Buchet-Chastel, Paris 1967

De Cecco, Manuela, *Non volendo aggiungere altre cose al mondo,* in Flash Art n° 200, 1996

Dupuis, Jean François, *Histoire désinvolte du surréalisme,* Paul Vernont, Paris 1977, trad. It. *Storia disinvolta del surrealismo,* AAA, Udine 1996

Friedman, Yona, *Utopie realizzabili*, Quodlibet, Macerata 2003

Hollevoet, Christel, *Quand l'objet de l'art est la démarche, flânerie, dérive et autres déambulations*, «Exposé» n° 2, Orléans 1995

Hollevoet, Christel, *Déambulation dans la ville, de la flânerie et la dérive a l'apprehnsion de l'espace urbain dans Fluxus et l'art conceptuel*, «Parachute» n° 68, 1992

Huizinga, Johan, *Homo Ludens*, Amsterdam-Leipzig 1939, trad. It. *Homo Ludens*, Einaudi, Torino 1949

Jappe, Anselm, *Guy Debord*, Manifestolibri, Roma 1999

Lambert, Jean Clarence, *Les Arteurs*, «Opus International» 17, 1970

Lambert, Jean Clarence, *Les Arteurs ou le dépassement de l'art*, «Opus International» 22, 1971

Lambert, Jean Clarence, *Constant. Les trois espaces*, cercle d'art, Paris 1992

Lambert, Jean Clarence, *New Babylon - Constant. Art et Utopie*, Cercle d'art, Paris 1997

La Pietra, Ugo, *Abitare la città, ricerche, interventi, progetti nello spazio urbano dal 1962 al 1982*, Alinea, Firenze 1983

Le Bon, Laurent edited by, *DADA*, Centre George Pompidou, Paris 2005

Lippolis, Leonardo, *Urbanismo Unitario*, Testo & Immagine, Torino 2002

Lippolis, Leonardo, *La nuova Babilonia. Il progetto architettonico di una civiltà situazionista*, Costa & nolan, Milano 2007.

Luther, Blisset, *Bugarrigarra - un confronto tra la psicogeografia e il 'Walkabout' degli aborigeni australiani* in "Luther Blisset" 1-2, Grafton, Bologna, giugno-settembre 1995

Marelli, Gianfranco, *L'ultima Internazionale*, Bollati Boringhieri, Torino 2000

Martin, Jean Hubert, *Dérives. Itinéraires surréalistes, dérives et autres parcours*, in AA. VV. «Cartes et cartographie de la Terre», Centre George Pompidou, Paris 1980

Nuvolati, Giampaolo, *Lo sguardo vagabondo. Il flâneur e la città da Baudelaire ai postmoderni*, Il Mulino 2006

Parinaud, André, *André Breton - Entretiens*, Gallimard, Paris 1952, trad. It. *Entretiens*, Schwarz, Milano 1960, Erre Emme, Roma 1991

Perniola, Mario, *I Situazionisti*, Manifestolibri, Torino 1972; Castelvecchi, Roma 1998

Perniola, Mario, *Appunti per una storia dell'urbanistica labirintica*, in "Rivista di Estetica" n°2, 1968

Prestinenza, Puglisi Luigi, *This is Tomorrow, avanguardie e architettura contemporanea*, Testo & Immagine, Torino 1999

Ricaldone, Sandro, *Jorn in Italia. Gli anni del Bauhaus Immaginista*, Fratelli Pozzo, Moncalieri 1997

Rumney, Ralph, *Le Consul*, Edition Allia, Paris 1999

Sanouillet, Michel, *Dada a Paris*, Jean-Jacques Pauvert, Paris 1965

Sadler, Simon, *The Situationist City*, London, Cambridge-Mass. 1998;

Solnit, Rebecca, *Wanderlust. A history of walking*, Viking Penguin, 2000

Solnit, Rebecca, *Walking and Thinking and Walking*, in "Kunstforum, Aesthetik des Reisens", n° 136, 1997

Urlberger, Andrea, *Parcours artistiques et virtualités urbaines,* L'Harmattan, Paris 2003

Wigley, Mark, *Constant's New Babylon. The Hyper-Architecture of Desire*, Witte de With Center for Contemporary Art / 010, Rotterdam 1998

Land Walk

AA.VV., *Primitivism in 20th century art*, edited by Rubin William, MOMA, New York 1985

AA.VV., *Art et Nature*, «Ligeia» n° 11-12, Paris, 1992

AA.VV., *Art et Architecture*, edited by Laroque Didier e Robert Jean Paul, «L'Architecture d'Aujourd'hui» 284, 1992

AA.VV., *Art et Architecture*, «Les Cahiers du Musée National d'Art Moderne» 39, 1992

AA.VV., *Cheminements*, «Les Carnets du Paysage», n° 11, Actes – Sud / E.N.S.P., Paris 2004

Adams Dennis et Malone Laurent, *JFK*, Marseille, 2002

Battcock Gregory, *Minimal Art, a critical anthology*, Dutton & co., New York 1968

Besse Jean-Marc, *Quatre notes conjointes sur l'introduction de l'hodologie dans la pensée contemporaine*, in : *Cheminements*, « Les Carnets du Paysage », n° 11, Actes – Sud / E.N.S.P., Paris 2004

Brinckerhoff-Jackson, John, (1984), Descubriendo el paisaje autoctono (ed. Joan Nogué), Paysaje y Teorìa, Biblioteca Nuelva, Madrid 2010

Brinckerhoff-Jackson, John, *Landscapes. Selected Essays of J.B. Jackson*, University of Massachussetts Press, Boston 1970

Brinckerhoff-Jackson, John, *A sense of place, a sense of Time*, Yale University Press, New Haven

Bois, Yve-Alain, *Promenades Pittoresque autour de Clara-Clara*, in «Serra», Centre George Pompidou, Paris, 1983

Bois, Yve-Alain e Krauss, Rosalind (1997), *L'informe*, Bruno Mondadori, Milano 2003

Brayer, Marie-Ange, *Mesures d'une fiction picturale: la carte de géographie*, «Exposé» n° 2, Orléans 1995

Brayer, Marie-Ange edited by, *Cartographiques, Actes du colloque à l'Académie de France à Rome 19-20 mai 1995*, RNM, Paris 1996

Brown Julia, *Michel Heizer. Sculpture in Reverse*, Los Angeles, 1984.

Buci-Glucksmann, Christine, *L'oeil cartographique de l'art*, Galilée, Paris 1996

Calvino, Italo, *Il viandante nella mappa*, in "Collezione di sabbia", Palomar/Mondadori, Milano 1984

Cardiff, Janet, *A survey of works including collaboration whit Georges Bures Miller*, P.S.1 Contemporary Art Center, Long Island City, New York 2001

Celant, Germano, *Michael Heizer*, Fondazione Prada, Milano 1996

Clement, Gilles, *Manifesto del Terzo paesaggio*, Quodilibet, Macerata 2005

Codognato, Mario, *Richard Long*, Electa, Milano 1994

Criqui, Jean-Pierre, *Ruines à l'envers: introduction à la visite des monuments de Passaic par Robert Smithson*, «Cahier d'Art. Musée National d'Art Moderne» n° 43, 1993

Cummins, Louis, La dialectique Site / Non-Site. Une utopie cartographique, "Parachute" n° 68, 1992

Flam, Jack, editor, *Robert Smithson, The collected writings*, University of California Press, Berkeley Los Angeles London 1996

Fried, Michael, *Art and Objecthood,* "Artforum" giugno 1967

Fuchs, Rudy H., *Richard Long*, Thames and Hudson, London and Solomon Guggenheim Foundation, New York 1986.

Fulton, Hamish, *Camp Fire*, Stedelijk Van Abbemuseum, Eindoven 1985

Fulton, Hamish, *One Hundred Walks*, Haags Gementemuseum, Den Haag 1991

Fulton, Hamish, *Walking beside the River Vechte*, Stadtische Galerie Nordhorn 1998

Fulton, Hamish, *Keep Mooving,* Museion Bolzano, Charta, 2005

Garraud, Collette, *L'idée de nature dans l'art contemporain*, Flammarion, Paris 1994

Gilchrist, Maggie e Boulan Marie-Sophie, Robert Smithson, *Le paysage entropique 1960-1973*, Avignon 1994

Krauss, Rosalind, *Passages in Modern Sculpture* (1981), tr. It. *Passaggi, Storia della scultura da Rodin alla Land Art*, Bruno Mondadori, Milano 1998

Krauss, Rosalind, *The Originality of Avant-Garde and Other Modernist Mytes*, M.I.T. Press, Cambridge Mass. (1985), trad. Fr. *L'originalitè de l'avant-garde et autres mythes modernistes*, Macula, Paris 1993

Krauss, Rosalind (1981), Passaggi. Storia della scultura da Rodin alla Land Art, Bruno Mondadori, Milano 1998

Lebovici, Elizabeth, *Land Art, le point de vue d'Icare*, «L'Architecture d'Aujourd'hui» 284; 1992

Lippard, Lucy, *Overlay, Contemporary art and the art of preystory*, Pantheon Books, New York, 1983

Lippard, Lucy, *Tony Smith*, Thames & Hudson, London 1972

Meneguzzo, Marco, *Il luogo Buono: Richard Long*, P.A.C., Milano 1985

Mock, Roberta, Walking, *Writing & Performance. Autobiografical text by Deidre Heddon, Carl Lavery and Phil Smith*, Intellect Bristol, UK/ Chicago, USA, 2009

Joan, Nogué (ed.), La construcciòn social del Pajsaje, Paysaje y Teoria, Biblioteca Nueva, Madrid 2007

Penders, Anne-Francoise, *En Chemin, le Land Art*, tome I : *Partir*, tome II : *Revenir*, La lettre volée, Bruxelles 1999

Poinsot, Jean-Marc, *Richard Long. Construire le Paysage*, "Art Presse", novembre 1981

Popper, Frank, *Art Action and Participation*, Studio Vista, London 1975

Seymour, Anne, *Richard Long. Piedras*, Madrid 1986

Seymour, Anne, *Richard Long: Walking in circles*, New York 1991

Szeemann, Harald edited by, *When attitudes becomes form*, Kunsthalle, Berne 1969

Taniguchi, Jiro (1992), *L'uomo che cammina*, Planet manga, 1999

Tiberghien, Gilles A., *Land Art*, Carré, Paris 1993

Tiberghien, Gilles A., *Sculptures Inorganiques*, in: «Les Cahiers du Musée National d'Art Moderne» n° 39, 1992

Tiberghien, Gilles A., *Le principe de l'axolotl & suppléments*, Crestet centre d'art, Strasbourg 1998;

Tiberghien, Gilles A., *Nature, art et paysage*, Actes Sud / École nationale supérieure du Paysage / Centre du Paysage, Paris 2001

Tiberghien, Gilles A., *Hodologique* in : *Cheminements*, « Les Carnets du Paysage », n° 11, Actes – Sud / E.N.S.P., Paris 2004

Tortosa, Guy, *In situ - In visu. Six jours dans le Tarn*, Cimase et Portique, Albi 1997

Tortosa, Guy, *Jardins ready-made et jardins minimaux*, in «Le jardin art et lieu de la mémoire», édition de l'Imprimeur, Besançon 1995

Varnedoe, Kirke, *Contemporary explorations*, in: William Rubin, "Primitivism in 20th-Century Art", MOMA, New York 1985

Wagstaff, Samuel, *Talking with Tony Smith*, "Artforum", December 1966

Transurbance

AA.VV., *Architettura della sparizione, architettura totale*, "Millepiani" 7, Mimesis, 1995

AA.VV., *Territoires Nomades*, «Inter Art Actuel» 61, Québec 1995

AA.VV., *Nowhere 1&2. Walking and Thinking and Walking*, Louisiana Museum, Copenhague 1996

AA.VV., *Itaten. Indagine sulle trasformazioni del territorio italiano*, Bari 1996

AA.VV., *Città - Natura*, Palazzo delle Esposizioni, Palombi, Roma 1997

AA.VV., *Suburban Discipline*, edited by Lang Peter, Princeton Architectural Press, New York 1997

AA.VV., *La ville, le jardin, la memoire*, Villa Medici, Charta, Roma 1998

AA.VV., "Art Press" n° 243, fèvrier 1999

AA.VV., *Neobabylonians*, "Architectural Design" vol. 71, n°3, 2001

AA.VV., *Francis Alys*, Musée Picasso d'Antibes/RMN, Lyon 2001

AA.VV., *Modos de acer. Arte, critico, esfera publica y action directa*, Universidad de Salamanca 2001

AA.VV., *Promenaden / Promenades*, "Topos" n° 41, Callewey, München 2002

AA.VV., *User's Manual for the Creative Disruption of Everyday Life*, MassMoCa, MIT Press, New York 2004

AA.VV., *Em Transito, Mobilidade e vida urbana*, Goethe Institut Lissabon, Lisboa 2004

AA.VV., *Babel 2. Diritto alla città*, Creative Commons License, Roma 2012

Adams, Dennis and Malone, Laurent, *JFK*, Marseille 2002

Almarcegui, Lara et Tiò-Bellido, Ramon, *Lara Almarcegui. Démolitions, wastelands, allotment gardens,* Etablissements d'en face et Le grand Café, Bruxelles et Saint-Nazaire, 2003

Ardenne, Paul et al, *Pratiques Contemporaines. L'art comme expérience*, Dis Voir, Paris 2000

Ardenne, Paul, *Un art contextuel*, Flammarion, Paris 2002

Augé, Marc, *Non-lieux: Introduction à une anthropologie de la surmodernité*, Seuil, Paris 1992. tr. It. *Nonluoghi: Introduzione a una antropologia della surmodernità*, elèuthera, Milano 1993

Auster, Paul (1985), *Trilogia di New York*, Einaudi, Torino 1996

Batty, Michael e Longley, Paul, *Fractal Cities: A Geometry of Form and Function*, Academic, San Diego 1994

Bey, Hakim, *T. A. Z., The Temporary Autonomous Zone*, Autonomedia, 1985, trad It. *T.A.Z. Zone temporaneamente autonome*, Shake, Milano 1991

Berenstein, Jacques Paola, *Estètica da ginga: A arquitectura dad favelas através la obra de Hélio Oiticica*, Casa da Palavra, Rio de Janeiro 2001

Basilico, Gabriele e Boeri, Stefano, *Sezioni del paesaggio italiano*, Art&, Udine 1997

Boeri, Stefano, Secchi, Bernardo e Piperno, Livia, *I territori abbandonati*, Compositori, Bologna 1990

Boeri, Stefano, Lanzani Arturo e Marini Edoardo, *Il territorio che cambia*, Abitare/Segesta, Milano 1993

Borden, Iain, Rendell Jane, Kerr Joe, Pivaro Alicia edited by, *The Unknown City. Contesting architectural and social space*, the MIT Press, Cambridge / London 2001

Burckhardt, Annemarie et Burckhardt, Lucius, *Barbecue City. Spaziergangswissenschaft in Bordeaux / Promenadologia a Bordeaux*, in: AA.VV., "Mutations", Arc en Reve, Bordeaux 2001

Lucius, Burckhardt, *Le design au-delà du visible*, Centre George Pompidou, Paris 1991

Careri, Francesco, *Rome archipel fractal, voyage dans les combles de la ville*, «Techniques & Architecture» n° 427, 1996

Careri, Francesco e Romito Lorenzo, *Stalker and the Big Game of Campo Boario*, in Blundell Jones Peter, Petrescu Doina and Till Jeremy edited by, "Architecture and Participation", Spoon Press – Taylor & Francis Group, London 2005

Careri, Francesco, Jean Marc Besse e Gilles Tiberghien, *Bande Itinerante: Stalker a la Praille*, Institut D'architecture Université de Genève, Genève, 2005

Careri, Francesco, *L'apartheid dei Rom e dei Sinti in Italia*, "Urbanistica Informazioni" n° 238, pp. 23-25

Careri, Francesco, *Of Sailing and Stopping*, in Marc Schoonderbeek (ed.), *Border Conditions*, A&NP – Architecture and Nature Press and TU Delft, Amsterdam 2010, pp.221-227

Cohen-Crux, Jan (edited by), *Radical Street Performance. An International Anthology*, Routledge, Londres/New York, 1998

Corboz, André, *Il territorio come palinsesto*, "Casabella" n° 516, 1985

Criconia, Alessandra, *Figure della demolizione*, Costa & Nolan, Genova-Milano 1998.

Davila, Thierry, *Marcher Creer*, Editions du regard, Paris 2002

Delgado, Manuel, *Elogi del vianant. Del "Model Barcelona" a la Barcelona real*, d'aquesta edicò de 1984, Barcelona 2005

Detheridge, Anna, *Visioni inattuali della città selva*, "Il Sole 24 Ore", 27 aprile 1997

Desideri, Paolo, *La città di latta*, costa & nolan, Genova 1995

Desideri, Paolo e Ilardi, Massimo edited by, *Attraversamenti*, costa & nolan, Genova 1997

Foucault, Michael, *Eterotropia, luoghi e non-luoghi metropolitani*, "Millepiani" n° 2, 1994

Foucault, Michel, *Spazi altri. I luoghi delle eterotropie*, mimesis, Milano 2002

Frankhauser, Pierre, *La fractalité des structures urbaines*, Collection Villes, Anthropos, Paris 1994

Giartosio, Tommaso, *L'O di Roma. In tondo e senza fermarsi mai*, Laterza, Bari 2012

Glissant, Edouard, *Poétique de la Rélation. Poétique III*, Gallimard, Paris 1990

Godfrey, Mark (ed.), *Francis Alÿs, a Story of deception*, Tate Modern, London 2010.

Herzog, Werner, *Sentieri nel ghiaccio*, Milano, Guanda, 1980

Hocquard, Emmanuel, "*Taches Blanches*", in *Ma Haie. Un privé à Tanger II*, P.O.L., Paris, 2001

Hughes, Jonathan and Sadler, Simon, *Non-Plan: Essays on Freedom Participation and Change in Modern Architetcture and Urbanism*, Oxford University Press, London 2000

Ilardi, Massimo, *La città senza luoghi*, costa & nolan, Genova, 1995

Ingersoll, Richard, *L'internazionale del turista*, "Casabella" 630-631, 1996

Indovina, Francesco, Matassoni Francesco, Savino Michelangelo, Sernini Michele, Torres Marco, Vettoretto, Luciano, *La città diffusa*, Stratema Collana R - Ricerche e Convenzioni n.1, luglio 1990

Labucci, Adriano, *Camminare, una rivoluzione*, Donzelli, Roma 2011

Lefebvre, Henry, *The production of space*, Basil Blakwell, Oxford 1991

Lefebvre, Henry, *Il diritto alla città*, Venezia - Padova, Marsilio, 1970

Lynch, Kevin, *The Image of the City*, M.I.T. Press, Cambridge-Mass 1960, trad. It. *L'immagine della città*, Marsilio, Venezia/Padova 1985

Lugon, Olivier, *Le marcheur. Piétons et photographes au sein des avant-gardes*, «Etudes Photographiques» n° 8, novembre 2000

Lyotard, Jean François, *Periferie*, "Millepiani" n° 2, 1994

Maspero, François, *Le passager du Roissy-Express*, Seuil, Paris 1990

Pasolini, Pier Paolo, *La lunga strada di sabbia*, (fotografie Philippe Séclier), Contrasto, 2005

Petti, Alessandro, Arcipelaghi e enclave, Bruno Mondadori, Milano 2007

Pernet, Alexis, *L'idée du bord*, «Le Carnet du Paysage» n° 7 automne 2001, Acte Sud et Ecole Nationale Supérieure de Paysage, Versailles 2001

Romito, Lorenzo, *Stalker*, in: AA.VV. "Suburban Discipline" edited by Lang, Peter, Princeton Arch. Press, New York 1997

Romito Lorenzo, *Ecouter, interagir*, in "Mutations", Arc en Reve, Bordeaux 2001

Romito, Lorenzo, "Walking out of Contemporary," in Mitrasinovic M.(Ed.), *Concurrent Urbanities: Designing infrastructures of Inclusion*, Routledge, 2015.

RoToR, Terrae, Water Air, manuals (2001 – 2008), dispari & dispari, 2009

Rowe, Colin, and Koetter, Fred, *Collage City*, Il saggiatore, Milano 1981

Secchi, Bernardo, *Analisi delle strutture territoriali*, Angeli, Milano 1965

Secchi, Bernardo, *La periferia*, "Casabella" n° 583, 1991

Scott-Brown, Denise, *Learning from Pop*, "Casabella" n° 359-360, 1971

Sennett, Richard, *The Uses of Disorder. Personal Identity and City Life*, New York 1970

Sinclair, Iain, *London Orbital, a piedi attorno alla metropoli*, il saggiatore, (London 2002) Milano 2008

de Solà Morales, Ignasi, *Urbanité Interstitielle*, «Inter Art Actuel» 61, Québec 1995

de Solà Morales, Ignasi, *Terrain Vague*, «Quaderns» n° 212, Barcelona 1996

Stalker, *Le Stazioni*, in: Desideri Paolo e Ilardi Massimo edited by, *Attraversamenti*, costa & nolan, Genova 1997

Stalker, *Attraverso i Territori Attuali*, Jean Michel Place, Paris 2000

Stalker, *Stalker / Ararat*, in "5tudi" ed. Dedalo, Roma 2000

Stalker, *Stalker*, capcMusée d'art contemporain de Bordeaux, Fage, Lyon 2004

Venturi, Robert, and Scott-Brown, Denise e Izenour Steve, *Learning from Las Vegas*, M.I.T. Press, Cambridge-Mass. 1972, trad. It. *Imparando da Las Vegas*, Cluva, Venezia 1985

Villani, Tiziana, *I cavalieri del vuoto. Il nomadismo nel moderno orizzonte urbano*, Mimesis, Milano 1992

Wenders, Wim, *L'atto di vedere*, Ubulibri, Milano 1992

Zardini, Mirko, *Paesaggi Ibridi*, Skira, Milano 1997

Photo Credits

p. 120: Georges Maciunas [et. al.] *Free Flux Tours,* 05/1976. Courtesy of Jon Hendricks. The Gilbert & Lila Silverman Fluxus Collection, Detroit.

p. 121: Bruce Nauman, Slow Angle Walk (Beckett Walk), 1968. Musée Picasso, Antibes. VEGAP.

p. 138: Vito Acconci, *Following Piece,* 3-25/10/1969, activities New York City, various locations. Courtesy Barbara Gladstone Gallery.

p. 139: Walter de Maria, film *Two Lines, Three Circles in the Desert,* 1969, Mojave, California, courtesy of Dia Center for the Arts, NY.

p. 140: Dennis Oppenheim, *Ground Mutations-Shoe Prints,* 1968. Collection Museum of Fine Arts, Houston, courtesy of Dennis Oppenheim.

p. 141: Stanley Brouwn, *This Way Brouwn,* Amsterdam, 25-26/02/1961.

p. 142: Dani Karavan, film *Dunes, Water and the Venice Biennale 1976,* courtesy of Dani Karavan.

p. 143: Christo, Wrapped Walk Way, courtesy of Christo & Jeanne-Claude. © Christo 1978. Photo Wolfgang Volz, VEGAP.

p. 149, 150, 151: Robert Smithson, *The Monuments of Passaic,* 1976. Sucession Robert Smithson, courtesy of John Weber Gallery, New York, VEGAP.

p. 158: © Stalker, Planisfero Roma, courtesy Stalker Nomad Archive.

p. 167–169: Lorenzo Romito and Romolo Ottaviani, Stalker Attraverso i Territori Attuali, courtesy Stalker Nomad Archive.

Acknowledgments

First of all, I would like to thank Mònica Gili and Daniela Colafranceschi for having made my driftings public. Particular thanks to Franco Zagari and Gianpiero Donin for their indications of the path of landscape in the territories of architecture, and Alessandro Anselmi for having pointed to the menhirs and the ways of Dada in those zones. A "merci beaucoup" to the Institut d'Arts Visuels d'Orléans for the invitation to help their students get lost, to Didier Laroque and Gilles Tiberghien for their precious advice during the Parisian phases, and to Yves Nacher and Guy Tortosa for always encouraging me to wander off into the forest. Affectionate thanks to Cristina Ventura, with whom I shared beautiful adventures amidst the stones of Sardinia, and to Paolo Bruschi and Lorenzo Romito, with whom I have playfully roamed many a byway. I would also like to thank Studiofrankus, a safe haven for arrivals and departures, the Ararat that is the final landing place, and Stalker, a case in which more than thanks are in order: in October 1995 we found ourselves tangled for five days in the brambles of the first transurbance in Rome. I decided to write this book to try to explain that first step to myself.

Index

Made in the USA
Coppell, TX
12 February 2025

45830204R00115